JACKSON HOLE, WYOMING

UNIVERSITY OF OKLAHOMA PRESS : NORMAN

David J. Saylor

JACKSON HOLE,
WYOMING

In the Shadow of the Tetons

Library of Congress Catalog Card Number: 70-123342

Copyright © 1971 by the University of Oklahoma Press, Publishing Division of the University, Norman. Manufactured in the U.S.A. First edition, 1971; second printing, 1977; third printing, 1982.

To the memory of my parents,

Tillman K. Saylor, Jr., and
Peggy Berkebile Saylor.

*They gave to their children
the priceless gift of unselfish love.*

PREFACE

It was as a small boy watching a nature program on television that I first heard the name Jackson Hole and marveled at the valley's fantastic scenery and wildlife. Since then I have spent two wonderful summers in Jackson Hole as a National Park Service employee and parts of several others as a tourist. This book is a testament of my love for the country.

Many of the tales of mountain men and Indians which comprise the first part of this volume have been told before in books on the fur trade. I have critically and exhaustively re-examined these works and the primary sources on which they are based in order to provide, I hope, the most complete and accurate account yet published of Jackson Hole's involvement in the western fur-trapping era.

In the second part, I have tried, among other things, to

provide a picture of life in what was a fairly typical western valley undergoing settlement. The courage and industry of those men and women who transformed a wilderness into a prosperous and progressive community ought to inspire people everywhere. And the lessons of justice, equality, and law and order which the early Jackson Holers learned through their pioneer experience are as valid today as they ever were.

In the third part, the story of the fight to save Jackson Hole from commercial destruction is told for the first time in its entirety. I believe it holds a vital message for present-day America, with her ever more crowded population centers, polluted skies and waterways, billboard-lined thoroughfares, and rapidly disappearing natural resources. Just as it was necessary in Jackson Hole in the 1920's, so is it imperative all across America today to act immediately and effectively to conserve the irreplaceable gifts of nature.

I am fortunate to have had the assistance of a number of wonderful people in preparing this history. My uncle, Congressman John P. Saylor, with the aid of his administrative assistant, Ann Dunbar, located research material and photographs and suggested many people who could help me in my task. In addition, his achievements as a leading conservationist in the U.S. House of Representatives were a constant source of inspiration during the writing of the third section.

Professor Frederick Rudolph of Williams College read the first two parts and an earlier version of the third and, through his wise counsel and incisive criticism, taught me much about the writing of history. Also at Williams, Mrs. Nancy MacFadyen secured needed information through the interlibrary lending service.

Former National Park Service Director Horace M. Albright and attorney Harold P. Fabian read the third chapter. With their wealth of personal experiences in Jackson Hole, they were able to suggest important additions and revisions. At the Park Service headquarters in Washington I was assisted by many people, most notably Harthon L. Bill, Frank E. Harrison, Elmer V. Buschman, and Diane Cole.

I am indebted to all of these people and to my talented typists, Bessie Wright in Williamstown, Massachusetts, and Pat Beblar in Johnstown, Pennsylvania. I also express my appreciation to the appropriate authorities for the use of the following research facilities: Library of Congress; National Archives; Department of the Interior Library; Grand Teton National Park Library; Coe Library, University of Wyoming; Widener Library, Harvard University; and Stetson Library, Williams College.

I want to thank my fellow employees on the maintenance crew at Grand Teton National Park for their friendship and encouragement. Part of my love for Jackson Hole surely derives from the pleasant associations I have had with these people.

Finally, I thank the members of my family for their patience, enthusiastic support, and abiding sense of humor, which kept me on the right track during the completion of this project. In particular, I am grateful to my father, who, in his characteristically unselfish manner, frequently indicated how much he wanted his son to become an author. I only regret that he did not live to see this book in print.

DAVID J. SAYLOR

Cambridge, Massachusetts

CONTENTS

ILLUSTRATIONS

Color

Black and White

Maps

Part I **EXPLORATION AND EXPLOITATION**

CHAPTER ONE

TOPOGRAPHY AND INDIANS

Hidden deep in the rugged recesses of the Rocky Mountains lies a spectacular mountain valley rich in history and simple in name. Men call it Jackson Hole.

The story of this valley is really the story of the American West in miniature. Across its sagebrush flats, along its rolling rivers, and beneath its snow-capped peaks have traveled and settled many of those remarkable characters who made the West what it was and is. Indians and trappers, gold seekers and surveyors, cattlemen and farmers, moviemakers and tourists, have all been eyewitnesses to the spellbinding beauty and the exciting history of Jackson Hole.

Jackson Hole is situated in the northwestern corner of Wyoming, south of Yellowstone National Park. Much of the fifty-mile-long, eight-mile-wide valley is now included in Grand Teton National Park. The fur trappers of the

3

1820's called the valley a hole because of its resemblance to a huge flat-bottomed cavity dug in the mountainous terrain which borders it on every side. To the north are the Yellowstone and Shoshone Highlands of the Absaroka Range; to the east, the Wind River Range, the Mount Leidy Highlands, and the Gros Ventre Range; to the south, the Wyoming Range; to the southwest, the Snake River Range; and to the west, the Teton Range.

In the north end of the valley, nestled at the foot of the Tetons, is Jackson Lake. Flowing south from the mouth of the lake is the mighty Snake River, which is joined by three major tributaries from the east: the Buffalo, Gros Ventre, and Hoback rivers. From Jackson Lake to the southern portion of Jackson Hole, the Snake rolls madly along, braiding its channels, cutting its meandering trench in the vast sagebrush flats, and collecting snowmelt from the mountains on either side. At the south end of the valley, the Snake cuts a deep canyon through the Snake River Range and flows out into Idaho and on to the Columbia.

The landscape in the north-central portion of Jackson Hole is dominated by the rugged Teton peaks, which rise abruptly, without benefit of foothills, from the flat valley floor. The highest is the Grand Teton (13,766 feet), towering a mile and a quarter above the sagebrush flats. With its deep glacier-carved cleavages, robes of fir and pine, and six sparkling gemlike lakes at its feet, the Teton Range is one of the most scenic mountain groups in the world.

Millions of years ago when the Tetons and the valley were linked together at the same elevation, the earth was broken by a north-south fracture near the eastern base of today's mountains. Through the slow course of time, the block of earth on the west side moved upward, all the while subjected to wind and water erosion. Meanwhile, the east block was depressed. The sedimentary strata on the steep side of the west block eventually washed down onto the east block, thus exposing the metamorphosed Pre-Cambrian rock which formed the interior of the west block. Millions of years earlier, the Pre-Cambrian rock had been sediment and volcanic matter deposited on the earth's surface. As the earth's crust evolved, the Pre-Cambrian layers were covered with other sediment and subjected to tremendous heat and pressure. Hot gases and liquids invaded the mass of meta-morphosing rock and solidified. The vertical black dikes on Mount Moran and the Middle Teton date from this era.

As the west fault block rose, streams cut canyons through it. During the more recent ice ages, glaciers flowed east through these canyons to coalesce with great ice sheets coming down from the north. Overlapping layers of glacial till and outwash deposits in present-day Jackson Hole sug-gest several separate glacial advances. One filled the basin to a depth of a couple of thousand feet. Hanging U-shaped canyons formed where mountain glaciers encountered the deep mass of ice in the valley. A later glacial advance excavated Jackson Lake. Similarly, glaciers in the canyons of the Tetons deposited the terminal moraines which now impound Leigh, Jenny, Bradley, Taggart, and Phelps lakes.[1] Today, a few retreating glaciers are visible high up on the Tetons.

The earliest evidence of man's presence in Jackson Hole consists of Indian arrowheads, grinding stones, and other artifacts uncovered in recent years along the northern shore of Jackson Lake.[2] Traces of Indian camps have been dis-covered along Spread, Mosquito, and Game creeks.[3] An early settler, Cal Carrington, claimed to have found a stone blind constructed by the Indians in Flat Creek Canyon.[4]

The red men probably did not spend their winters in

5

Jackson Hole because of the severe cold and deep snows, but they certainly visited the valley during the warmer months to hunt the antelope, elk, and buffalo that roamed through the region. The Indians entered Jackson Hole over high mountain passes or through steep river canyons, often leaving crudely marked trails along the way. From the headwaters of the Yellowstone in the north, they crossed to Two Ocean Pass on the Continental Divide, descended Pacific Creek, and were soon in view of Jackson Lake. In the northeast, they came over Togwotee Pass between the Absaroka and Wind River ranges and traveled down Black Rock Creek to the Buffalo River. In the east, they used Union Pass in the Wind River Range as a gateway to the Gros Ventre River Canyon. From the southeast, they ascended the Green River, climbed to the Hoback Rim, and descended the Hoback River Canyon. In the south, they occasionally risked the steep-walled Snake River Canyon. The Teton Range blocked them in the west except for two passes, one through the southern end of the range, known as Teton Pass,[5] and the other through the northern end at the headwaters of Berry Creek, known as Conant Pass.

Each Indian tribe in the Rocky Mountain region had a favorite habitat. To the northeast of Jackson Hole lay the homeland of the Absarokas, or Crows, expert horsemen and even better horse thieves. To the south and west lived the Shoshonis, or Snakes. Northwest of Jackson Hole was the domain of the Flatheads and Nez Percés, peace-loving nomads who, according to ancient Indian lore, once flattened their heads and pierced their noses. More than a hundred miles north of Jackson Hole dwelt the fierce Blackfeet, hated neighbors of the Flatheads and vicious antagonists of the first white men in the Rockies.[6]

One band of the Blackfoot tribe, the Atsinas, or Gros

Ventres of the Prairie, made annual pilgrimages southward to visit their former neighbors, the Arapahoes, who lived along the South Platte River in present-day Colorado. Each spring, the Gros Ventres packed up their tents at the headwaters of the Missouri and set out for the Platte, often passing through Jackson Hole on the way. The Gros Ventre Range on the east side of Jackson Hole was probably named for these Indians, who frequently camped along its base and hunted in its forests while making their yearly visit to the Arapahoes.[7]

One small group of Indians may actually have endured the rugged winters of Jackson Hole. The Tukuarika band of the Shoshonis, known as Sheep Eaters, was scattered throughout the mountainous regions of northwestern Wyoming.[8] This shy, backward people owned no horses, subsisted on roots and small animals and occasional mountain sheep, and lived in caves and under huts high up in the mountains. Though no written or archaeological records have been discovered that conclusively prove the presence of Sheep Eaters in Jackson Hole, it is quite probable that at some time in the distant past they did live there.[9]

CHAPTER TWO

JOHN COLTER

As they pursued the daily tasks that had occupied them for centuries, the Indians living in and around Jackson Hole could hardly have guessed that their future would be vastly altered by a squat, balding emperor on the other side of the world. In 1803, Napoleon Bonaparte agreed to sell the Louisiana Territory to the United States. Though Jackson Hole lay just outside the boundaries of the Louisiana Purchase, the early history of white men in the valley begins with the expedition sent by President Thomas Jefferson to explore the newly acquired territory.

In the company of the Meriwether Lewis and William Clark exploring expedition (1803–1806) was a Virginia-born hunter named John Colter, who hired on at Maysville, Kentucky, October 15, 1803, for a fee of five dollars a month.[1] Thomas James, a contemporary, described Colter

8

as being five feet ten inches tall and possessed of "an open, ingenious, and pleasing countenance of the Daniel Boone stamp."[2] Colter accompanied Lewis and Clark up the Missouri, across the Rocky Mountains of present-day Montana and Idaho, and down to the Columbia and the Pacific. On the return trip, Clark and some of the men made a loop to the south along the Yellowstone River while Lewis, Colter, and the others kept to the north along the Missouri.

In the entry for August 12, 1806, Lewis' journal reveals that not far below the juncture of the Yellowstone and the Missouri, the party came upon "the camp of two hunters from the Illinois [River] by name Joseph Dickson and Forest Hancock," who had been trapping on the Lower Yellowstone and the Missouri. After providing Dickson and Hancock with a description of the beaver areas they had seen on the Upper Missouri, Lewis and company rejoined Clark. An hour later, though, Dickson and Hancock reappeared and received permission to accompany the now combined groups down the Missouri to the Mandan Indian villages in present-day North Dakota.[3]

A day after the group reached the villages, Dickson and Hancock persuaded John Colter to take leave of the expedition, turn his back on civilization, and return to the wilderness of the Rockies with them. Clark recorded the incident:

Colter one of our men expressed a desire to join Some trappers (the two Illinois Men we met, & who now came down to us) who offered to become shearers with [him] and furnish traps &c. the offer [was] a very advantagious one, to him, his services could be dispenced with from this down and as we were disposed to be of service to any of our party who had performed their duty as well as Colter had done, we agreed to

9

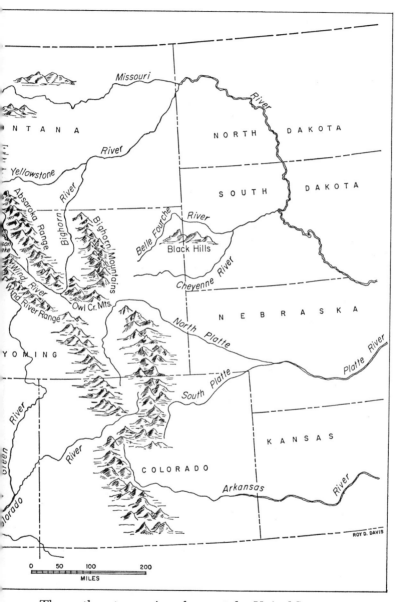

The northwestern region of present-day United States

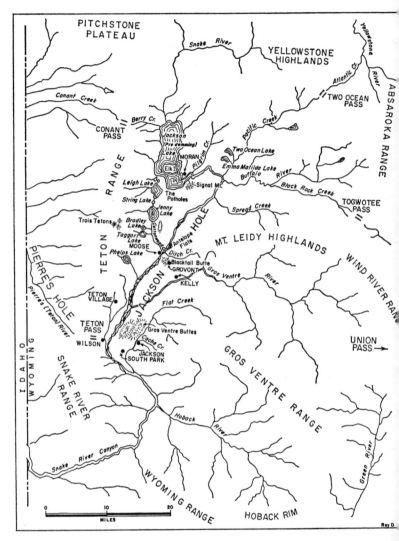

Jackson Hole

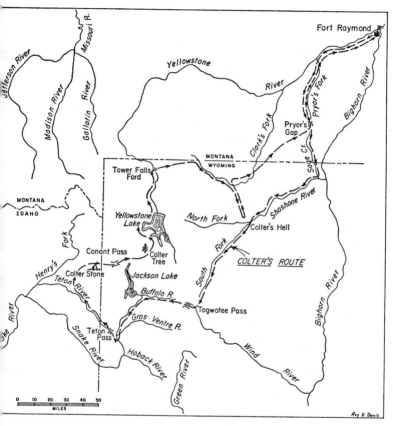

John Colter's probable route in 1807 and 1808

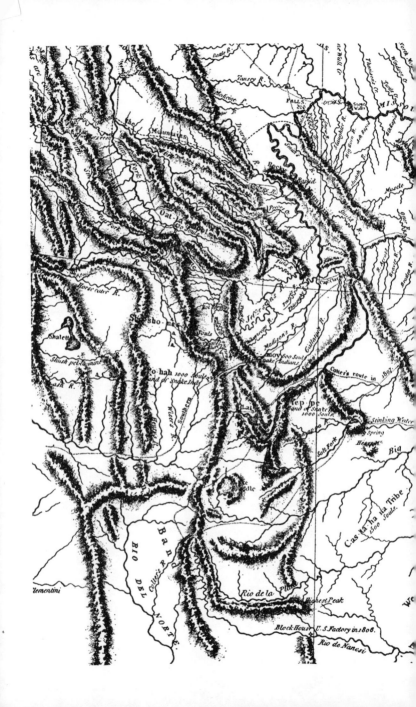

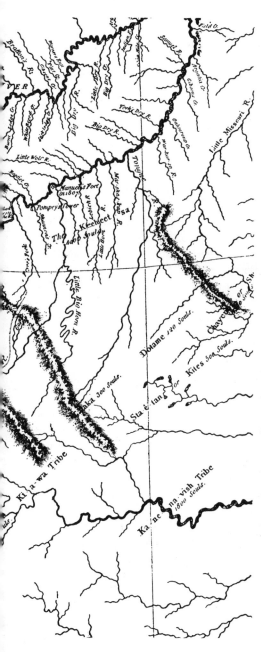

Samuel Lewis' map showing John Colter's route in 1807 and 1808. From James K. Hosmer (ed.), *History of the Expedition of Captains Lewis and Clark*, Chicago, 1902, Vol. I, following page 124.

allow him the privilage provided no one of the party would ask or expect a Similar permission to which they all agreed that they wished Colter every suckcess and that as we did not wish any of them to Separate untill we Should arrive at St. Louis they would not apply or expect it. . . . we gave Jo Colter Some Small articles which we did not want and some powder & lead. the party also gave him several articles which will be usefull to him on his expedition.[4]

On August 17, 1806, Colter and his partners set out up the Missouri.

The three men must have reached the beaver country of the Upper Missouri and the Yellowstone sometime in the fall of 1806. Exactly where they trapped and how successful they were will never be known. Unfortunately, none of the three kept a journal or penned a letter concerning the expedition. After wintering in the mountains, they dissolved their partnership and headed back toward civilization. Traveling alone in a canoe, John Colter floated down the Missouri toward St. Louis. Near the mouth of the Platte, several hundred miles above St. Louis, Colter met Manuel Lisa and a party of trappers heading for the same spot Colter had so recently left. Lisa encouraged him to join the group, and he consented, thus turning his back on civilization once more.[5] Whether it was Lisa's promise of monetary reward or simply the "call of the wild" that persuaded Colter to return to the wilderness cannot be determined. Probably both factors played a part. In any case, he had joined an expedition that would soon send him where no civilized man had ever been before. Thanks to his fateful decision at the mouth of the Platte, John Colter was destined to become the first white man to visit Jackson Hole.

Manuel Lisa was one of the first people in St. Louis to

The "Colter Stone," reputedly carved in 1808 by John Colter, the first white man to visit Jackson Hole

Jim Bridger's beaver trap

Les Trois Tetons from Hurricane Pass

For the Rocky Mountains.

THE subscribers wish to engage One Hundred MEN, to ascend the Missouri, to the

Rocky Mountains,

There to be employed as Hunters. As a compensation to each man fit for such business,

$200 Per Annum,

will be given for his services, as aforesaid.— For particulars, apply to J. V. Garnier, or W. Ashley, at St. Louis. The expedition will set out from this place, on or before the first day of March next.

Ashley & Henry.

jan 18.   40tf

Administrator's Notice.

THE undersigned having taken out letters ...

Advertisement in the *St. Louis Enquirer*, January 25, 1823, which lured Davey Jackson into the fur trade

The celebrated trappers' ford on the Snake River south of Jackson

The Cunningham barn, near Spread Creek, where a posse killed two suspected rustlers in 1893

T BRITAIN

ation to Submit
tion.

OB VIOLENCE

ndon Hotel Torn
e Protection
n Pablo's
te.

New-York Times.
a Galveston, July
eetings have been
ble against Great
authority in the

en made denounc-

ondon Hotel, in
yesterday by the

moned to protect
San Pablo from

London has se-
t that Great Brit-

dad's Location.

to arbitration the
ip of Trinidad,
by Brazil.
e Times will to-
patch from Rio
protest has been
e direct Argentine
rinidad.
t the Chamber of

STRIKERS OF PANAMA ARE PACIFIC

The Government Is Able to Suppress Riots
That May Occur and the Railroad
Company Has Men at Work.

Special Cablegram to The New-York Times.
PANAMA, via Galveston, July 26.—A report that the United States Government was
discussing the advisability of sending a
warship to Colon to protect American interests there causes the general expression
of opinion here that such an act would not
be justified by the condition of affairs.
The strikers are entirely pacific. No disorder has occurred since their strike began.
The Government is quite capable of sup-
pressing any riots that may happen.
There is a veteran garrison here of about
600 men. The Panama Railroad Company
has 140 men at work.
At Colon the strike is expected soon to
collapse.
The steamer Santiago's departure for the
south has been delayed until Saturday because of the strike.

THE DISPUTE OF ITALY AND COLOMBIA

President Cleveland, as Arbitrator,
Will Consider Claims in October.

WASHINGTON, July 26.—One of the first
matters of public interest to engross President Cleveland's attention after his return
to Washington, in October next, will be a
consideration of the dispute between the
kingdom of Italy and the republic of Colombia, growing out of damages sustained
by a subject of the former country during
a revolution in Colombia in 1885. The
amount claimed is between $800,000 and
$700,000.
A voluminous correspondence passed between the Foreign Offices of the two countries without any agreement being reached.
It was finally suggested by Colombia that
the dispute be referred to President Cleveland for arbitration. The Italian Government at once agreed to the proposition, and
a protocol was shortly afterward signed.
President Cleveland was asked in February last if he would fill the role of arbitrator, and after due consideration gave
his consent. Both Governments felicitated
themselves upon the President's acceptance,
as he is regarded, not only as an excellent
lawyer, but as a painstaking, conscientious
man, whose conclusions will be rendered
only after a thorough examination of all the
papers submitted to him.

WANTS THE GOLDBUGS CRUSHED

Senator Butler Says Andrew Jackson
Ought to be Alive in These Times.

TIRZAH, S. C., July 26.—A three days'
encampment of the State Alliance is under
way here. Senator Marion Butler of North
Carolina, in the opening speech, said the
currency question had become so serious
that the masses must form a new party
and fight.
"Would to God," he exclaimed, dramat-
ically, "we could call up Andrew Jackson
to-day from his grave to lead these people
against the same enemies that he fought
and thought he had crushed, to hurl ad-
fiance at and crush the goldbugs!"
Senator Tillman addressed about 2,500
persons. His speech was a reproduction of
the one he delivered at the silver convention
at Memphis. He said the time had come
for putting aside the livery of the Democratic Party, and for forming a coalition
of the forces of the South and West to over-
come the combined North and East.

SENATOR HILL COMES TO TOWN

Visit to Gen.

SETTLERS MASSACRED

Indians Kill Every One at Jackson's Hole.

COURIER BRINGS THE NEWS

Red Men Apply the Torch to All
the Houses in the Valley.

ALARM IN THE SURROUNDING COUNTRY

Another Messenger with Details of
the Successful Ambuscade
Is on the Way.

U. S. TROOPS ARE NEARING THE SCENE

They Can Reach the Place Sunday
Night—Gen. Coppinger in
Command.

POCATELLO, Idaho, July 26.—A courier
who arrived at Market Lake, Idaho, this
evening reports that all the settlers in
Jackson's Hole have been murdered by Indians and all the houses burned.
He could give no particulars of the alleged massacre. He said that a companion
had attempted to reach the scene of the
trouble. If he escaped the Indians he would
undoubtedly reach Market Lake within
twenty-four hours, with details of the fight.
M. J. Gray, L. M. Tart, and Senator
Hamer of Illinois, and T. R. Hamer of St.
Anthony, all left St. Anthony Wednesday
morning on a fishing trip to Jackson's Hole,
taking no stock in the Indian war. They
are back to-day and report every man,
woman, and child in Jackson's Hole murdered.
A courier who has just returned, got far
into Teton Basin, which is the present point
in danger of massacre, now that Jackson's
Hole citizens are all butchered. He reports
that the smoke of a large fire can to-day be

seen several miles south of Grand Te
the direction of Jackson's Hole.
There is no doubt that the redskin
fired every home and cabin. By m
they will be repeating their work th
of the Teton range in Teton Basi
perhaps after that all down the Teton
Valley in Idaho.
Two hundred Utes were reported t
gone north to join the Indians in I
Basin early this week. Small part
Lemhi's men have been slipping i
across the Conant trail, somethin
have not ventured to do since the Y
stone National Park was enlarged in
People in St. Anthony, Rexburg
other towns located in Idaho, betwe
railway and Jackson's Hole, have b
along placing no confidence in the
dian scare," as they called it. The
now changed their minds.
Market Lake is 120 miles from Jac
Hole.
Signal fires can be seen blazing t
in the mountains, and it is stated o
authority that the Indians now off t
ervation have sent back the ponies
away with them for more braves wh
doubtless slip away to-night unles
are closely watched, and they probal
be allowed to do as they please.
The statement has been made her
Agent Teter is really the man who
sponsible for the present troubles, as
been in the habit of allowing the bu
leave the reservation whenever they
His kindness to the redmen, it is s
due to the fact that under the law
dian off reservation draws no ratior
Pleasure seekers who have been sp
some time in the neighborhood of th
oles are now on their return home
well-known that the settlers are well
while the Indians, unless they have
supplies lately, have not the amm
they desire. This is probably the
why news of a decisive battle had n
received before this. A band of ba
nocks led by a disreputable white m
to join the reds yesterday.
OMAHA, Neb., July 26.—The news
massacre of the settlers in Jackson
is confirmed by the Union Pacific R
officials. A telegram was received s
from the Superintendent at Marke
that the Indians have killed every
and that the stock was slaughtered.

SETTLERS PREPARED FOR

Bought Up All the Ammunitio
Have 1,000 Rounds Each

SALT LAKE, Utah, July 26.—Th
of the killing of twenty whites at J
Hole Tuesday still lacks confirmati
it is believed to be a canard.
A telegram from Pocatello says:

Report of the "massacre" at Jackson Ho

evidence of the thorough manner in
both the settlers and the Indians in
ackson's Hole Valley are preparing for
continues to arrive every day. Ike
a traveling man of Salt Lake, arrived
atello last night, having come di-
from a trip through the portion of
unty south of the Yellowstone Na-
Park, in which the bushwhacking
gn is being carried on between hos-
settlers and ambushed Indians.
all learned that there are seventy-five
of families in the Jackson's Hole

two weeks they have been prepar-
the condition that now exists. In
to forestall the Indians messengers
ent to buy up all the ammunition
could be obtained in that section of
untry, and they now have on hand
100 rifles, and every settler is sup-
ith 1,000 rounds of ammunition. The
now expressed that when the Indians
the troops are surely coming
may endeavor to make a sudden
and then make all haste for the res-
ns, and, by the time the regulars
re, they will be peaceably lounging
ir accustomed haunts."

ERNMENT NOT ALARMED.

**re the Bannock Indians Will
Soon Give Themselves Up.**

HINGTON, July 26.—It is believed
War Department that the troubles
n the settlers in Wyoming and the
ck Indians will soon be ended. The
that were ordered to the scene of
ons have been hurried forward as
possible, and the delays that usually
n such cases have been obviated to
e extent.

egram received to-day by Assistant
en. Vincent stated that Gen. Cop-
would arrive at Market Lake, Idaho,
night to-night, and the troops at an
hour to-morrow morning. Market
is 120 miles from the scene of the

Gen. Schofield arrived in the city
'clock this evening and will devote
ention from now on to the suppres-
the Bannocks. Gen. Schofield had
ws to communicate regarding the in-
roubles.

n Commissioner Browning to-day re-
a telegram from Agent Teter, the
Hall Agent, stating that the Indian
agers sent out yesterday to convey
ommissioner's telegrams urging the
oks to return to their reservations
eported to 'him that the Indians de-
to do so. Agent Teter has requested
sion of the Commissioner to accom-
the troops to the scene of the
e. He will be allowed to do so.

AN AGENT BECK SUSTAINED.

**ion of Tenants of the Flournoy
rom the Reservation Approved.**

HINGTON, July 26.—The actions of
Beck, United States Army, Indian
of the Omaha and Winnebago Indi-
as been approved by the Department
Interior in the matter of evicting
ants of the Flournoy Land Company
he lands of the Indians.

g Secretary Reynolds of the Interior
ment, late this afternoon, replied to
egram of the Nebraska Congres-
delegation stating that the depart-
approved of the manner in which
Beck had proceeded, as it was in ac-
ce with the decision of the United
Circuit Court at St. Louis, Mo., that
lournoy Company leases were ille-
cting Secretary Reynolds suggested
delegation that the settlers could
themselves by taking out leases

INJUNCTION FOR O'BRIEN

Aqueduct Board Restrained from Let-
ting the Reservoir Contract.

CONTRACTOR SAYS GEN. DUANE LIES

**The Lie Returned by the General, Who
Says He Never Had a Conversa-
tion Alleged — Scott
Explains.**

John O'Brien, the contractor, began active
warfare yesterday on the Aqueduct Commissioners in the Jerome Park reservoir
matter. Through his counsel, Browne &
Sheehan, he obtained a temporary injunction from Justice O'Brien of the Supreme
Court restraining the Commissioners from
letting the contract to John B. McDonald,
who was declared the successful bidder last
Wednesday on his offer to do the work for
$5,472,080.

Argument on the motion to make the injunction permanent will be heard next
Thursday in Supreme Court, Chambers.
Corporation Counsel Scott will appear for
the Aqueduct Commissioners, and ask to
have the injunction vacated, while Mr.
O'Brien's lawyers will ask to have it made
permanent on the ground that the Commissioners could not legally let the work to
Mr. McDonald, but to give the contract to
Mr. McDonald offer to do the work for $174,710 less.

The injunction proceedings came in the
nature of a surprise, and it was very generally said yesterday that Mr. O'Brien's
lawyers had stolen a march on the Commissioners. Ex-Judge Browne obtained
forty-eight hours on Wednesday to file a
protest against the final award of the contract to Mr. McDonald, in order that the
Corporation Counsel might pass on the
question, and it transpired yesterday that
this time had been employed to get the
papers in shape on which the injunction
was secured, which completely ties the
hands of the Commissioners until the courts
can pass on the case.

That the matter will be fought most bitterly on both sides was made plain by the
papers submitted to Justice O'Brien, and
by the statements made to a reporter for
The New-York Times by the interested parties. The lie was passed yesterday between
Gen. James C. Duane, President of the
Aqueduct Board, and Mr. O'Brien, both gentlemen embellishing their defiance with
strong adjectives. Speaking of an affidavit
made by Mr. O'Brien and presented to the
Supreme Court Justice, Gen. Duane said:

"John O'Brien is a liar!"

Mr. O'Brien, when informed of this, grew
furiously angry, and declared:

"Duane is a liar! Yes, Sir, a liar; an un-
qualified liar, and he knows it, and I can
prove it!!"

The affidavit that called out this exchange,
of personalities reads, in part:

Deponent (O'Brien) further says that he believes that the award of said contract to John
B. McDonald was not made or considered as a
public act by the said defendant Commissioners,
but was influenced and directed among other
things, by personal prejudice and caprice of some
of the said Commissioners, and that deponent's
conclusion is based upon the following conversation had with Mr. Duane, the President of said
board, at the office of said Aqueduct Commissioners, on or about the 18th day of July, 1895.
That in such conversation said Duane stated to
deponent:

And' said Duane asked deponent if he (deponent) could not get some one to arrange it
for him with Cannon. If deponent could, then,
Mr. Duane said, deponent could get the contract.
That he (Duane) had had a conversation with
Cannon and that said Cannon said to Duane
that under no circumstances would he (Cannon)
vote to give the contract to O'Brien, and that
he (Cannon) had a personal prejudice against
O'Brien, and that he would resign rather than
vote to award the contract to O'Brien. Said
Duane further stated to deponent that if deponent could get Commissioner Cannon "off "
or would remove his personal prejudice, that
then Commissioner Tucker would vote with said
Duane. That deponent asked Duane if there
was any objection to deponent because of his
connection with the construction of the aqueduct. Duane said that there was not; that there
could not be any objection to that, as it had
been accepted and was all done satisfactorily.

Deponent further says that conversations occurred just prior to the day assigned for the
first meeting of the commission after the bids
were received for the work. That, although a
meeting was fixed for said day, the Commissioners did not meet in public session, and thereafter
and before the meeting at which said award was
made, and after the bids were made, it was
generally rumored in and about the offices of
said Aqueduct Commissioners that deponent
would not be awarded said contract. That deponent was informed by Andrew McMillan, a
bidder for said work, which information deponent believes to be true, that two gentlemen
named Drake and Stratton were interested in
the bid of said John B. McDonald.

"I never had a conversation with O'Brien
in my life about the reservoir contract,"
Gen. Duane asserted when the substance of
this affidavit was submitted to him, and
after he had stigmatized the assertion as a
lie. "I have seen the man since the matter
has been up for bids only once, and then
I ran across him in the office of our chief
engineer, with whom he was apparently going over the plans. I left the office at once
and went into my own room, and I suppose
he went away at once after finishing his
business with the chief engineer."

"Gen. Duane said that, did he!" Mr.
O'Brien asked when told of this statement
by the head of the Aqueduct Board. Mr.
O'Brien devoted himself to the task of returning the "lie," and then he added:

"On the occasion referred to by Duane
he came into Chief Engineer Fteley's office,
where I was. I hailed him, and said I
wanted to speak to him. He said he would
see me in his office, and after I finished my
business with Mr Fteley, I went in there
and we had the conversation I have detailed. The attendants in the office can testi-
fy to that, for they saw me with Gen.
Duane. I thought so well of the advice that
Gen. Duane gave me as to Mr. Cannon
that I sent at once to that gentleman, as
the General suggested, but I found that I
could do nothing with Mr. Cannon, who
seemed to have his mind fully made up.
That Gen. Duane should now deny our conversation is simply outrageous, though in
perfect keeping with his reputation for veracity."

Another statement made by Mr. O'Brien
in connection with the controversy relates
to a conversation he had with Corporation
Counsel Scott. This statement is attached
to the formal protest or brief against the
letting of the contract to Mr. McDonald,
which Mr. O'Brien submitted to the Aqueduct Commissioners in conformity with the
understanding of Wednesday. In it he says:

Before presenting his bid for the building of
the Jerome Park reservoir, and on or about July
8, 1895, he (O'Brien) called on Francis M. Scott
at the Corporation Counsel's office and talked
with him about the bid he contemplated making
for the building of the reservoir. He asked the
Corporation Counsel if there was any objection to
his bidding for the work, or if the Aqueduct
Commissioner entertained a prejudice of any
kind against him. If such a prejudice existed
Mr. Scott would certainly have known of it, as
he had been for years an Aqueduct Commissioner, and had only recently retired from the
board.

In answer to my inquiry, Mr. Scott said that
there could be no objection to my bidding for
the work; that I was not in default in any way
in any way; that I had carried out all agreements made by me with the city, and that no
prejudice existed against me, unless Commissioner Cannon was unfriendly, and the Corporation Counsel advised me to see Commissioner
Cannon, saying that if Cannon was all right he
believed the rest of the Commissioners would be.
The Corporation Counsel furthermore made me

Jackson Hole from Teton Pass

recognize the economic possibilities of the territory explored by Lewis and Clark. Spanish by heritage but American by terms of the Louisiana Purchase, he dreamed of an empire of permanent trading posts strung out along the Upper Missouri and its tributaries. Lisa and his two partners, William Morrison and Pierre Menard, intended to dispatch parties of traders from these posts to secure furs from the Indian tribes of the region. According to Lisa's plan, the Indians would do most of the trapping and Lisa's men would trade with the red men and transport the furs to St. Louis.[6]

After an eventful trip involving encounters with three hostile Indian tribes and the murder (at Lisa's request) of an employee who tried to desert, Lisa's keelboats turned off the Missouri and headed up its tributary, the Yellowstone, as far as the mouth of the Bighorn River. There Lisa constructed his first wilderness trading post, named Fort Raymond (or Rémon) for his son but known also as Manuel's Fort.[7]

In November, 1807, while the fort was still under construction, Lisa asked John Colter to seek out the Indian villages scattered along the streams south and west of the fort. Colter was instructed to acquaint himself with the topography of the region and to invite the Indians to bring their furs to the trading post.[8] Why Lisa sent Colter out so late in the year, with extremely cold weather and heavy snowfalls expected soon, is unclear. Undoubtedly he was anxious to inform the Indians of his new enterprise before the spring trading season began. Certainly Colter, a veteran of one winter in the Rockies, knew the danger of traveling alone in the treacherous cold and snow. Whatever the case, he accepted the challenge.

Colter's route from Fort Raymond has become a matter

of great controversy. He kept no journal, and if he drew any maps, none has survived to the present day. The best clue to the mystery surrounding his lonely trek is a dotted line, marked "Colter's route in 1807," on a map in Nicholas Biddle's history of the Lewis and Clark Expedition published in 1814.[9] The map was compiled in Philadelphia by Samuel Lewis (no relation to Meriwether Lewis), who based his work on drawings and maps sent to him by William Clark. Clark learned about Colter's travels from Colter himself when the latter returned to St. Louis in 1811. Clark sent Samuel Lewis a sketch of Colter's route to supplement his own drawings of the Rocky Mountains and asked Lewis to work the information into a composite map of the West.[10] Earlier, he had sent Lewis the original (or a copy) of a map drawn by another former employee, George Drouillard, who had made two trips up the Bighorn River for Lisa in 1808.[11] When Lewis (certainly with Clark's help) attempted to integrate all of this information into a single map, he mistakenly connected several of the streams and mountain ranges explored by Colter to totally different streams and mountain ranges explored by Drouillard. The resulting topographical confusion makes any reconstruction of Colter's route somewhat conjectural.

Several possible routes have been suggested.[12] That theory which has Colter passing through Jackson Hole, over the Tetons to Pierre's Hole (present-day Teton Basin, Idaho), and back through the mountains to northern Jackson Hole and parts of Yellowstone Park is the most defensible, thanks to the discovery of two Colter-made relics along that route.

After leaving Fort Raymond, Colter apparently traveled up the Yellowstone to Pryor's Fork, which he ascended to its source. From there he crossed a divide (Pryor's Gap) and descended a tributary (present-day Sage Creek) of the Stinking Water (Shoshone) River (Samuel Lewis erred when he drew the stream descended by Colter as a tributary of the Bighorn). Upon reaching the Stinking Water, Colter turned upstream, where he discovered a "boiling spring" (see Lewis' map). Known in trapper lore as Colter's Hell,[13] the "spring" was confused in later years with the hot springs and geyser basins now enclosed in Yellowstone Park. Recent investigations, however, have identified Colter's Hell as a once-active thermal area, Demaris Springs, not far from present-day Cody, Wyoming.[14]

Colter left his "Hell," continued up the South Fork (Salt Fork on Lewis' map) of the Stinking Water, and crossed a low divide down into the Wind River Valley by way of Du Noir Creek. There he undoubtedly encountered wintering Indian tribes, spread the news about Lisa's fort, and engaged an Indian guide to show him the easiest pass over the next range of mountains. A remark Colter made a few years later to Henry M. Brackenridge provides a clue to the nature of the particular mountain pass selected by the guide. Brackenridge maintained in 1811 that within a certain region of the Rocky Mountains at

the head of the Gallatin Fork [Yellowstone?] and of the Grosse Corne [Bighorn River] . . . discoveries since the voyage of Lewis and Clark . . . [reveal that the Rockies are] less difficult to cross than the Allegheny mountains [of Pennsylvania]. Colter, a celebrated hunter and woodsman, informed me that a loaded wagon would find no obstruction in passing.[15]

Brackenridge's account sounds very much like a description of Togwotee Pass, which is, in fact, a fairly easy wagon route. Although one cannot be certain, Colter probably

27

took the old Indian path over Togwotee Pass and down Black Rock Creek into Jackson Hole.

As he descended from Togwotee Pass, Colter must have been struck by the extraordinary winter beauty of Jackson Hole. Spread out before him was a broad, snow-blanketed valley dotted with forested buttes and guarded in the distance by the soaring peaks of the Teton Range. There was probably no campfire smoke visible at that end of the valley, so Colter trudged toward the southern portion of Jackson Hole, hoping to find friendly Indians camped there. When he encountered no one at the south end and saw the high mountains which blocked his path farther in that direction, he turned west toward a low point on the Teton Range, now known as Teton Pass. He picked his way through the deep snow, forded the icy, turbulent Snake River, crossed some more flat land, and ascended Teton Pass to the summit, where he looked out onto another beautiful snow-covered expanse: Pierre's Hole.

Colter descended into Pierre's Hole, where he encountered several streams, one of which was labeled "Colter's River" on Samuel Lewis' map. It was probably a tributary of the Snake River. Since Colter had not seen the canyon cut by the Snake as it flows west through the mountains, he assumed that the stream in Pierre's Hole was part of a river system entirely distinct from the one he had seen in Jackson Hole. On Lewis' map, the rivers in Jackson Hole were mistakenly connected to Bighorn River, which flows east and north. Lewis (or his informant, Clark) evidently assumed that Colter's River was a tributary of the Río del Norte, the mythical northern waters of the Río Grande, and connected Colter's River to it on the map. The headwaters of the Río Grande were, in fact, several hundred miles to the south and separated from Colter's River by high mountain barriers.

Colter apparently journeyed north through Pierre's Hole and made camp at a spot three and a half miles east of present-day Tetonia, Idaho. On this spot in 1931, home-steader William Beard and his son discovered a stone, carved in the likeness of a man, bearing on one side "JOHN COLTER" and on the other side the date "1808." On display at the Grand Teton National Park Museum in Moose, Wyoming, the stone is composed of rhyolite lava, a substance that is relatively easy to carve. Fritiof Fryxell, a noted geologist, historian, and park ranger, carefully studied the Colter Stone after its discovery and concluded that it could not be a fake.[16] Because it matched the outcroppings of near-by rock, the stone had probably not been transported to the spot. The Beards claimed not to have heard of John Colter. If they are taken at their word, then, they were not perpetrating a hoax. The stone was partly buried when it was found. If someone other than the Beards had intended a hoax, it seems unlikely that he would have buried it and risked the possibility that it would never be discovered.[17]

Fryxell examined the edges around the facial features, the name, and the date and determined that the carved edges had weathered a great deal. Such weathering, which could not have been accomplished by human hands, proved to Fryxell that the stone had been exposed to the eroding powers of wind and water for quite some time. Certain people have doubted the authenticity of the date because Samuel Lewis' map marks Colter's route "in 1807." Quite probably, failure to affix "–1808" was simply another of the many errors Lewis made in compiling his map.

Having left Fort Raymond in November, 1807, Colter

could not possibly have walked all that distance in the snow to Pierre's Hole and returned to Fort Raymond before the end of December, 1807. Other writers have erroneously argued that the Colter Stone is a relic of a later Colter trip in 1808. On that journey, Colter reputedly helped the Crows and Flatheads repel an attack by the Blackfeet. H. M. Chittenden, who was not a contemporary of Colter, mistakenly placed the Indians' battle in Pierre's Hole.[18] Thomas James, who was with Colter in 1810 when the latter revisited the battle site, placed it in the Three Forks area— where the Madison, Jefferson, and Gallatin rivers converge to form the Missouri—many miles north of Pierre's Hole.[19]

After carving his stone for posterity, Colter wandered northward until he found the Indian trail over Conant Pass, crossed the northern end of the Teton Range, and came out along the north shore of Jackson Lake. The lake, which he must have described later to William Clark, was labeled "Lake Biddle" on the Lewis map in honor of Nicholas Biddle, author of the first history of the Lewis and Clark Expedition and later president of the Second Bank of the United States. From Jackson Lake, Colter turned north into present-day Yellowstone National Park and followed upstream that narrow branch of the Snake River which flows south into the north end of Jackson Lake. Some distance farther he presumably turned off the Snake and up Coulter Creek. In 1889, not far from the bank of the creek, three men discovered Colter's initials carved on a tree. One of them, historian Philip Ashton Rollins, described the carving as follows:

> . . . on the left side of Coulter Creek, some fifty feet from the water and about three quarters of a mile above the creek's mouth, a large pine tree . . . [revealed] a deeply indented blaze, which after being cleared of sap

and loose bark was found to consist of a cross thus "X" (some five inches in height), and, under it, the initials "JC" (each some four inches in height).[20]

The other two men, John H. Dewing and Tazewell Woody, both expert woodsmen and the latter a hunting guide for Theodore Roosevelt, testified to the authenticity of the carving and estimated its age at close to eighty years. The tree was later cut down, and the carved section was sent to Yellowstone Park officials. It was lost in transit, however, and never recovered.[21]

From Coulter Creek, Colter headed north to the shores of Yellowstone Lake, which William Clark later named Lake Eustis for Secretary of War William Eustis. He passed around the western side of the lake and proceeded north along the Yellowstone River, which flows out of the lake. Colter discovered an Indian trail that crossed the river near present-day Tower Falls,[22] and from this ford he headed east, cross country, to Pryor's Fork and north to Fort Raymond. Lewis' map shows a short dotted line leading south from Colter's trail to the Stinking Water. This may indicate that Colter made a side trip back to the boiling spring on the Stinking Water and then doubled back to the trail he had followed after fording the Yellowstone. The dotted line could simply be a drafting error by Lewis or a misinterpretation by Clark. Colter told Clark about several hot springs he had seen along the Yellowstone on his return trip to Fort Raymond, and perhaps Clark thought Colter was referring to the boiling-spring region on the Stinking Water.

When Colter returned to Fort Raymond, the spring trading season had begun and some of the Indians he had visited were already exchanging their furs at the fort. Lisa was pleased with the prospects of the region and returned to St. Louis to collect men and supplies for the construction of more trading posts.[23] While Lisa was in St. Louis, Colter made several more trips into the unknown region west of the fort. The first, in the summer of 1808, involved the Indian battle mentioned earlier.[24] In this fight at the Three Forks of the Missouri, he earned the everlasting enmity of the Blackfeet by assisting their enemies, the Flatheads and the Crows, in a skirmish with the Blackfeet. The Blackfeet got their revenge a few months later when they captured Colter and another trader, John Potts, along a creek near Three Forks.[25] According to an account of the affair which Colter related to John Bradbury in 1811, Potts attempted to escape and was, in Colter's words, immediately "made a riddle of" by the Indians' arrows.[26] Colter himself was stripped naked and set up as a standing target, but a chief intervened before he could be executed. The chief told him that the Indians would give him a chance to run for his life. Colter may have had some difficulty understanding what the chief wanted him to do, but he soon took up the challenge and began to race across the flats toward the Jefferson River, six miles away. The Indians gave him a respectable head start and then, with a "horrid war whoop," took off in pursuit. After several miles across the prickly-pear–covered plain, he heard one of his spear-carrying pursuers "not twenty yards" behind him. Colter

> suddenly stopped, turned round, and spread out his arms. The Indian, surprised by the suddenness of the action, and . . . exhausted with running . . . fell whilst endeavoring to throw his spear, which struck in the ground and broke. . . . Colter instantly snatched up the pointed part, with which he pinned him [the Indian] to the earth, and then continued his flight.[27]

Colter reached the Jefferson River and plunged into the water moments before his screaming pursuers arrived on the scene. He swam underwater to a pile of driftwood that had become lodged in midstream and concealed himself beneath it until nightfall, when the Indians gave up the search. A week later, Colter stumbled naked, sunburned, and starving, into Fort Raymond. His feet were filled with prickly-pear thorns. The adventure sounds fantastic, but it may well be true. Thomas James, who spent considerable time with him in the mountains, maintained that Colter's "veracity was never questioned among us."[28] Lewis and Clark's journals recorded nothing but praise for his character.[29]

Back in St. Louis, Lisa's optimistic reports on his fur-trading enterprise greatly impressed prominent businessmen in that frontier river town. They decided to form a new trading concern, the St. Louis Missouri Fur Company, which consisted of eleven members, including Lisa and his two partners, Menard and Morrison.[30] The company purchased Fort Raymond from the Lisa-Menard-Morrison firm and outfitted an expedition to return to the fort. It left St. Louis in the spring of 1809 and arrived at Fort Raymond in the fall.[31] During that fall and winter, a profitable trading and trapping campaign was conducted. Some of the men may have retraced John Colter's steps into Jackson Hole. A tree blaze and inscription, "Ike Weeler Oct 17 1809," allegedly seen between Granite and Shoal creeks in Hoback Canyon, would indicate that at least one trapper visited Jackson Hole in 1809.[32]

On March 1, 1810, thirty-two men, including John Colter, Andrew Henry, Pierre Menard, and Thomas James, started overland from Fort Raymond to the Three Forks of the Missouri, where they intended to establish a second

33

trading post. According to James, the group experienced bitter cold, incredible suffering, and snowblindness. They passed the site of the battle between the Blackfeet and the Crows and Flatheads in which Colter took part.[33] The trappers built a post "on the neck of land between the Jefferson and Madison rivers, about two miles above their confluence."[34] Dispersed in small parties to trap beaver and to seek out the friendly Flatheads, they found the country filled not only with beaver but also with the treacherous Blackfeet, who were armed with rifles obtained from British and Canadian traders. On April 12, 1810, the Blackfeet ambushed a party of trappers and killed five. Several other parties were similarly attacked and robbed. The optimism which had pervaded the thinking of the company's field leaders was dissipated by this upsurge in Indian savagery. Menard left the country in fear and disgust. Even John Colter, after narrowly surviving several more encounters with the Blackfeet, decided to forego his love for the wilderness and return to civilization. He went back to Fort Raymond and from there took a canoe down the Yellowstone and the Missouri to St. Louis, where he married, settled down as a farmer, and died a few years later of jaundice.[35]

CHAPTER THREE

THE ASTORIANS AND THE NORTH WESTERS

Not all the men at Three Forks gave up. Andrew Henry decided to head south to the watershed of the Snake, where his men would be free of the Blackfoot menace. They crossed the Continental Divide and established a fort on the North Fork (marked Henry's River on Samuel Lewis' map) of the Snake River near present-day St. Anthony, Idaho.[1] About fifty years ago, a stone relic, with inscribed names of Henry and four of his compatriots and the date 1810+, was uncovered near the site of Henry's fort.[2]

During the fall of 1810, at least two of Henry's men, perhaps acting on information from their former companion at Three Forks, John Colter, entered Jackson Hole over Teton Pass,[3] trapped along its beaver-rich streams, and returned to Henry's fort by either Teton or Conant Pass. The post, which never consisted of anything more than a few crude

35

cabins, was abandoned in the spring of 1811 after a severe winter food shortage.

Henry and some of his men returned north via Three Forks to Fort Raymond, while the rest split into two groups, one turning south toward the Spanish colonies and the other heading east through Pierre's Hole and Jackson Hole.[4] In the small party traveling through Jackson Hole were John Hoback, Jacob Reznor, and Edward Robinson, two of whom had trapped in Jackson Hole the previous fall and probably desired to explore the valley some more. The three left Jackson Hole over Togwotee Pass[5] and worked their way to the waters of the Missouri, where, on May 26, 1811, they encountered an expedition of trappers under Wilson Price Hunt of the newly formed Pacific Fur Company. John Bradbury, an English botanist accompanying the expedition, records the arrival of the three trappers:

> Whilst at breakfast on a beautiful part of the river [Missouri], we observed two canoes descending on the opposite side. In one, by the help of our glasses, we ascertained there were two white men, and in the other only one. A gun was discharged, when they discovered us, and crossed over. We found them to be three men belonging to Kentucky, whose names were Robinson, Hauberk [Hoback], and Reasoner [Reznor].[6]

The trio agreed to guide the new company's expedition across the Rocky Mountains.

The Pacific Fur Company had been organized in 1810 by John Jacob Astor of New York as part of a scheme to exploit the fur resources of the Columbia and Missouri watersheds and to secure the land northwest of the Louisiana Purchase for the United States. Astor, who financed the project from his fortune accumulated in the Great Lakes fur trade, was an advocate of manifest destiny long before anyone had coined that term. According to Washington Irving, historian of the Pacific Fur Company venture, Astor wanted to establish a trading post on the Columbia River which would

form the germ of a wide civilization; that would, in fact, carry the American population across the Rocky Mountains and spread it along the shores of the Pacific, as it already animated the shores of the Atlantic.[7]

Astor intended to ship the furs collected on the Columbia to the great fur markets in China, just as he had shipped the products of his Great Lakes trade across the Atlantic to the European markets.

To accomplish Astor's grand commercial and colonial designs, the Pacific Fur Company sent two expeditions to the mouth of the Columbia River. One group sailed around Cape Horn on the ship *Tonquin,* carrying supplies for the proposed post on the Columbia. The land expedition, which was joined en route by Hoback, Reznor, and Robinson, was to proceed along the route followed by Lewis and Clark, "exploring a line of communication across the continent, and noting the places where interior trading posts might be established."[8]

Wilson Price Hunt, commander of the land expedition, did not follow the exact route of Lewis and Clark because of what he learned from his three new guides. Hoback, Reznor, and Robinson confirmed his worst notions about the warring Blackfeet who lived along the old Lewis and Clark trail. The trio suggested the route which they had taken earlier in the spring through Jackson Hole, bypassing the main Blackfeet villages to the north. Hunt agreed.[9] Because of its safe distance from hostile Indians, Jackson

37

Hole was now to become, in Merrill J. Mattes' words, the "crossroads of the western fur trade."[10]

After reaching the Arikara Indian villages along the Missouri in present-day South Dakota and there procuring eighty-two horses, Hunt's party, composed of six partners and associates; eleven hunters, interpreters, and guides; forty-five Canadian *engagés*; and one woman (an interpreter's wife) and her two small children, left the river for their long overland trek to avoid the Blackfeet. Because most of the horses were needed to carry packs, everyone but Hunt, the woman, her children, and a few others had to walk. The motley assemblage reached the Wind River Valley in early September and ascended the Indian trail to Union Pass. Hunt's diary records the event:

> One of our hunters [Hoback, Reznor, or Robinson], who had been on the shores of the Columbia, showed us three immensely high and snow-covered peaks [the Tetons] which, he said, were situated on the banks of a tributary [Snake River] of that river.[11]

Hunt named the three peaks Pilot Knobs because of their distinctive shape and significant location.

Hunt had originally planned to continue over the pass and down Gros Ventre Canyon into Jackson Hole, but, finding his meat supply low, he now headed south for the "Spanish [Green] River," where buffalo were reported to be abundant. After killing enough game for the long trip ahead, Hunt's expedition took the Indian trail up Hoback Rim and down into precipitous Hoback Canyon, where one of the horses "fell with his pack into the river from a height of nearly two hundred feet, but was uninjured." Somewhere along the way, the members of the expedition named this river the Hoback in honor of guide John Hoback, who had probably explored it the year before and had told Hunt about this alternate canyon route into Jackson Hole.

On September 27, 1811, Hunt's party arrived at the confluence of the Hoback and the Snake, which they appropriately named Mad River. Now that he had reached the watershed of the Columbia, Hunt hoped to travel the rest of the way by water. He sent three men downstream to ascertain the navigability of the Snake and put most of the remaining men to work constructing canoes.[12] Four employees, Alexander Carson, Pierre Delaunay, Pierre Detayé, and Louis St. Michel, were

> fitted out with traps, arms, ammunition, horses, and every other requisite, and were to trap upon the upper part of Mad River, and upon the neighboring streams of the mountains . . . . When they should have collected a sufficient quantity of peltries, they were to pack them upon their horses and make the best of their way to the mouth of Columbia River, or to any intermediate post which might be established by the company.[13]

Hunt and another man, perhaps Hoback, crossed the Snake and made a reconnaissance trip north through Jackson Hole for twelve miles. They saw "many indications of beaver, some signs of gray [grizzly] bear and a band of elk," but few trees suitable for dugout canoes.[14]

Two Snake Indians who came into Hunt's camp several days later advised him to abandon his plans for navigating the river and recommended the route west over Teton Pass. The three men sent downstream reported that navigation would be hazardous, whereas horse travel along the Snake River Canyon wall was impossible. Upon hearing their report, Hunt decided to cross Teton Pass and pick up the Snake on the other side, where he hoped it would be more navigable and large trees for building canoes more plentiful.

On October 4, the expedition forded the river, "the water being up to the horses' bellies," and camped at the foot of the Tetons. The next day, they climbed the trail to the snow-covered pass, descended into Pierre's Hole, and proceeded toward Henry's abandoned post. There five men— Joseph Miller, Martin Cass, Hoback, Reznor, and Robinson—"left to go beaver-trapping." The rest of Hunt's party attempted unsuccessfully to descend the Snake in canoes. One man was drowned in the icy rapids and several canoes carrying the expedition's meat were dashed to pieces on the rocks. Lost and faced with starvation, Hunt cached his goods and divided his party into four groups, which were to seek their way overland as best they could. After enduring incredible hardship, some of the men arrived on the Columbia in time to help those who had sailed around the Horn on the *Tonquin* finish construction of the Pacific Fur Company's trading post, Fort Astoria.[15]

In the spring of 1812, several trapping brigades left Fort Astoria with orders to explore the beaver-rich tributaries of the Columbia and Snake, establish small trading posts along these tributaries, and invite the local Indian tribes to the posts. At the same time, a party of six men, under the leadership of *Tonquin* veteran Robert Stuart, left Fort Astoria for St. Louis and eventually New York, where Stuart was to inform John Jacob Astor of the company's progress and obtain funds for additional operations on the Columbia watershed.[16] Stuart followed in reverse Hunt's approximate route through present-day Oregon and into the southeastern corner of what is now Idaho. In this area, southwest of Jackson Hole, Stuart encountered Joseph Miller, Hoback, Reznor, and Robinson, who, along with Martin Cass, had left Hunt at Henry's old fort the previous

The Erwin cabin, about 1927, on land later purchased by the Rockefeller interests

Bill Menor's ferry, built at Moose in 1892 and reconstructed in the
1940's by Jackson Hole Preserve, Inc., a Rockefeller corporation

The cabin of Elijah N. ("Uncle Nick") Wilson on Fish Creek, Wilson, the town named for him

Mount Owen above Cascade Creek

The Bar BC Ranch, a few miles north of Moose, on the west bank of the Snake River

View overlooking the western slope of the Tetons and Cascade Canyon Trail above Lake Solitude. Grand Teton is in the center.

Group of elk on the National Elk Refuge, Jackson, Wyoming

COURTESY NATIONAL PARK SERVICE

PHOTOGRAPH BY E. P. HADDON

The Joe Pfeiffer homestead, Mormon Row

fall to trap Pierre's Hole and the streams to the south. Between the time they had left Hunt and the time they met Stuart, the four men had trapped in Pierre's Hole and south along Bear River, had been robbed by the Arapahoes, journeyed east to the Green and Bighorn rivers, where Cass deserted them, and then returned to the Snake, perhaps by way of Jackson Hole.

The four men joined Stuart's party, and together they found Hunt's Snake River caches. Only three caches had escaped detection by the Indians, but from them Stuart obtained enough equipment to outfit Hoback, Reznor, and Robinson for another two years of trapping. Joseph Miller, his "curiosity and desire of travelling thro' the Indian countries being fully satisfied," chose to return immediately with Stuart to St. Louis.[17]

Not long after Stuart left them, Hoback, Reznor, and Robinson met John Reed and a Pacific Fur Company brigade en route from one of the recently completed interior posts to Hunt's caches on the Snake. In Reed's party were Alexander Carson, Pierre Delaunay, and Louis St. Michel, who, along with Pierre Detayé, had been dispatched by Hunt in Jackson Hole months before. After leaving Hunt, they had completed a successful trapping season in Jackson Hole and then headed north to the Three Forks of the Missouri. There a band of Indians had attacked and robbed them, killing Detayé. The three survivors had wandered on foot to a friendly Indian village, where Delaunay acquired a wife and where Reed discovered them. Carson, Delaunay, St. Michel, Hoback, Reznor, and Robinson returned with Reed to the Columbia and Lower Snake, where most of them later perished at the hands of the Indians.[18]

Meanwhile, Robert Stuart was heading southeast along a route discovered several months earlier by his new guide,

Joseph Miller, and Miller's former companions, Hoback, Reznor, and Robinson. Unfortunately, Miller had a poor memory and got Stuart's expedition lost along the Portneuf River in Idaho. Rather than continue stumbling through the wilderness, Stuart

> concluded that our best, safest and most certain way would be to follow the River down, and pass the first spur of mountains by the route of the Party [Hunt's] who came across the Continent last year . . . .[19]

Stuart turned north toward Henry's fort and Pierre's Hole, familiar ground for two of his men, Ramsay Crooks and Robert McClellan, both of whom had been with Hunt in 1811.

After they arrived in Pierre's Hole, McClellan grew impatient with Stuart's slow pace and apprehensive about the food supply; he left the main group and forged ahead over Teton Pass and into Jackson Hole. Stuart and his companions—Benjamin Jones, François Leclair, André Vallé, Crooks, and Miller—crossed Teton Pass several days later. On October 7, 1812, they camped along the Snake. The next day, they proceeded downstream along the east bank to the mouth of Horse Creek. In camp that night, Stuart "saw a great many Antelopes very wild—Killed none," and Vallé set the party's only beaver trap; the next morning, he retrieved a beaver from it.

The party continued south to the Hoback River, then east along its north bank. Six miles upstream, somebody shot a small buck antelope, part of which was mixed with Vallé's beaver and eaten that night. On October 10, the men continued up the north bank "along an abominable road occasioned by the proximity of the mountains where the track is often in places so nearly perpendicular, that missing a single step you would go several hundred feet into the rocky bed of the stream below." They camped near the confluence of the Hoback and Hunters Fork (present-day Jack Creek). The following day, they ascended Fish Creek, halted on the Hoback Rim near the cold campfire of Robert McClellan, and "went to bed without supper."[20]

Dropping down into the Upper Green River Valley the following morning, the six starving men searched desperately for the buffalo which Hunt had reported seeing there. Instead of buffalo, they found McClellan, "lying on a panel of straw worn to a perfect skeleton and hardly able to speak." That night, either Vallé or Leclair proposed that the men choose one of their number by lot to be killed and eaten by the others, but a horrified Stuart rejected the proposal. Strangely, that evening as he lay in bed close to death, Stuart mused over the democratic future of the West. "If the advocates for the rights of man come here," he wrote, "they can enjoy them, for this is the land of *liberty and equality*, where a man sees and feels that he is a man merely, and that he can no longer exist, than while he can himself procure the means of support."[21]

Luckily, the following afternoon, the seven starving Astorians "discovered an old run down Buffalo Bull," which they killed and whose meat they ravenously ate, swallowing "part of the animal raw." Saved from starvation, Stuart and company continued eastward, crossed "a gape discernable in the mountains"[22] (possibly the one known to Oregon Trail pioneers as South Pass), wintered on the Platte River, and arrived in St. Louis on April 30, 1813.

When Stuart reached St. Louis, he learned that Great Britain and the United States had been at war since June 19, 1812. He undoubtedly realized the threat which war posed to Astor's enterprise on the Columbia. Most of the

Pacific Fur Company's employees had been recruited from Canada and were loyal British subjects capable of surrendering Fort Astoria to the British without a fight. Months before, John Jacob Astor had asked the American government for naval protection around Fort Astoria. The government was unable to comply because all men and ships were needed along the Atlantic and on the Great Lakes.[23]

On October 23, 1812, long before Stuart reached St. Louis, Astor's worst fears were realized. With no American military or naval protection available and with the appearance of a British warship *Raccoon* expected daily, the men at Astoria chose to sell their fort rather than surrender it at gunpoint. It was purchased by the North West Company, a Montreal-based firm which for years had maintained trapping operations in western Canada and was now attempting to expand into the Columbia and Snake river regions. The North Westers renamed their acquisition Fort George and enlisted a good many former Pacific Fur Company employees to carry on the new enterprise.[24] Back in New York, Astor, who had not been consulted prior to the sale of his fort, vowed revenge on those who had wrecked his great plans for the Pacific Northwest.[25]

While the war progressed and Astor pondered various means of revenge, the North West Company launched several trading and fort-building campaigns in its new domain. But poor leadership, disciplinary problems, and Indian hostility over the next four years prevented the North Westers from reaching the richest of the former Pacific Fur Company lands—the Upper Snake River and Jackson Hole. In 1816, the situation changed. Donald McKenzie, veteran of Wilson Price Hunt's transcontinental expedition who was instrumental in negotiating the sale of Fort Astoria, was placed in charge of the North West Company's Snake River Division. Knowing from personal observation the great fur-producing potential of the Snake River region, including Jackson Hole, he led several trapping expeditions up the Snake to its source. Instead of following the normal North West Company practice of relying on Indians to do the trapping, McKenzie outfitted his own men with three hundred beaver traps.[26]

McKenzie's traveling notes, which "were often kept on a beaver skin, written hieroglyphically with a pencil or a piece of coal,"[27] have been lost to modern research. What is known of his Snake River expeditions has been gleaned from a secondary source, Alexander Ross's *Fur Hunters of the Far West,* published in 1855. Ross, a veteran of the *Tonquin* voyage hired by the North Westers in 1812, periodically met with McKenzie to discuss McKenzie's journeys. He quoted McKenzie as saying that on his first expedition (September, 1818, to February or March, 1819), several Iroquois[28] were left to trap along the "Skam-naugh" (Boise) River while the rest of the men were spread out in various groups along the Snake River and its environs.[29] McKenzie and six men[30] swung east and then north around the mountains to explore the headwaters of the Snake. Quite possibly, they reached Jackson Hole and the southern end of Yellowstone Park, where the true headwaters of the Snake are located. McKenzie reported to Ross that in the winter of 1818 to 1819,

> taking a circuitous route along the foot of the Rocky Mountains, a country extremely dreary during a winter voyage, I reached the headwaters of the great south branch [*i.e.,* the headwaters of the Snake, the south

53

branch of the Columbia], regretting every step I made that we had been so long deprived of the riches of such a country.[31]

Traveling through "many parts I had seen in 1811," McKenzie returned to the Iroquois trappers, who, to his dismay, had now moved east across the plains to several Indian villages, where they were searching for women instead of beaver. One of the Iroquois, Pierre Tivanitagon, had traversed the valley on the west side of the Tetons which now bears his name, Pierre's Hole.[32] While crossing it, he and some of his French-speaking companions had observed three snow-capped peaks on the mountainous horizon to the east. To the homesick, love-starved Iroquois, the peaks were Les Trois Tetons—The Three Breasts. The name Tetons has lasted to this day, having long ago supplanted Wilson Price Hunt's more sterile "Pilot Knobs."

After putting the Iroquois back to work trapping beaver, McKenzie returned on snowshoes to Fort Nez Percés, the North West Company post at the confluence of the Walla Walla and Columbia rivers. He made a second trip (April, 1819, to June, 1820) to check on his trappers along the Snake, but he probably did not enter Jackson Hole at that time. It is likely, however, that one of the men did visit Jackson Hole and the Yellowstone country to the north, for in 1880, Yellowstone Park Superintendent Colonel P. W. Norris found a trapper's inscription, "JOR   Aug 19 1819," carved on a tree a mile above the Upper Falls of the Yellowstone.[33] No other organized trapping parties are known to have been in this region at the time.

According to Ross, the Snake River expeditions were great financial successes, but apparently not great enough to enable the North West Company to fight off the encroaching power of a much older London-based firm, the mighty Hudson's Bay Company.[34] The North Westers and the Hudson's Bay people had been involved in ruinous competition for years. Rather than risk a complete financial fiasco, the North Westers agreed on March 26, 1821, to a merger.[35] The new firm, which retained the Hudson's Bay Company name, continued to expand operations in the Snake River area and in 1823 sent Finan McDonald, a red-bearded giant of a man, on a trapping tour that quite likely took him through Jackson Hole. Fourteen deserters from a Hudson's Bay expedition commanded by Michel Bourdon may have preceded McDonald through Jackson Hole in 1822.[36]

CHAPTER FOUR

HEYDAY OF THE BEAVER MEN

As the Canadians and British pushed deeper into the beaver regions of the Rocky Mountains, they inevitably heard of several new American companies that were beginning to trap beaver on the east side of the Continental Divide. One of them was a St. Louis–based firm founded in 1822 by General William H. Ashley, lieutenant governor of Missouri. He hoped to reopen areas which had lain virtually untouched by American trappers since the withdrawal of Lisa's St. Louis Missouri Fur Company in 1811. Joining him was Andrew Henry, Lisa's former partner and builder of the now abandoned fort on Henry's Fork of the Snake River in 1810.[1]

In 1822, Henry led the Ashley-Henry firm's first expedition up the Missouri to the mouth of the Yellowstone, where Fort Henry, consisting of a stockade and several buildings, was erected. He pushed on to Three Forks the following spring but was driven back by his old antagonists the Blackfeet. That same spring, 1823, Ashley led a second keelboat expedition upriver to meet Henry. After an early-morning attack by the Arikaras in present-day South Dakota, the survivors escaped downriver and met Henry at the mouth of the Cheyenne. Ashley returned downstream, while Henry took most of the men and equipment overland to Fort Henry.[2]

On the way to the Yellowstone, one of Henry's hunters, a tough old mountaineer named Hugh Glass, was jumped by a grizzly bear and nearly mauled to death.[3] Henry, over-due at the fort, left two men (one of whom may have been Jim Bridger, a mere youngster destined to become a great pioneer guide and army scout) to attend the dying Glass. The pair, left alone with a virtual corpse in the heart of hostile Indian country, deserted their unconscious comrade without waiting to give him a proper burial. Great was their surprise when, months later, they learned that old Hugh was still very much alive. Horribly mutilated and weak from loss of blood, he had regained consciousness and crawled more than a hundred miles to Fort Kiowa on the Missouri, "feasting" along the way on roots, berries, and wolf-killed carrion.[4]

Back on the Yellowstone, Henry built a new outpost, Fort Cass, near the mouth of the Bighorn and from there sent out a trapping party, which included one Daniel T. Potts.[5] Jedediah S. Smith, a Scripture-quoting young man of twenty-one, was at the same time leading a second party of trappers overland from Fort Kiowa.[6] The two parties evidently met and spent the winter together in the Wind River Valley, just east of Jackson Hole.[7]

The Ashley-Henry firm made several refinements and

innovations in the Rocky Mountain fur trade. They used roving trapper brigades instead of trading and fort-building parties. Like North Wester Donald McKenzie before them, Ashley and Henry disliked the practice of relying on Indians to do the trapping and white men to do the trading, transporting, and fort building. Products of a different culture, the red men did not appreciate the limitations which time and money imposed on a trapping enterprise. Indian trappers sometimes failed to produce sufficient quantities of high-quality furs just when white traders most urgently needed them. The Indians did not lack the skill to trap; they simply lacked the cultural stimulus to furnish furs on a consistent basis. Consequently, Ashley and Henry relied on more "dependable" white trappers. They also introduced the annual wilderness rendezvous, where trappers could exchange furs for equipment and promissory notes. Because forts were not needed at rendezvous sites, the fur companies saved the time and cost of their construction.[8]

In February, 1824, the Smith and Potts[9] parties, wintering among the Indians in Wind River Valley, attempted "to cross the mountains north of the Wind River [ra]nge but found the snow too deep—and had to" turn back.[10] Apparently, the trappers wanted to ascend either Togwotee or Union Pass in hopes of entering Jackson Hole. Andrew Henry, their boss, may have remembered reports from his men in 1810 and suggested Jackson Hole as a likely prospect for the 1824 brigades. Instead, the brigades traveled along the eastern base of the Wind River Range, crossed South Pass (for the first time since Robert Stuart used it in 1812),[11] and entered the Green River Valley. While most of the men began trapping and skinning beaver, Thomas Fitzpatrick and James Clyman set out for St. Louis to meet with Ashley and arrange for a rendezvous on the Green the following summer.

Jedediah Smith and six companions were sent west and north and eventually wound up on the Snake River watershed, where they observed Alexander Ross and his Hudson's Bay brigades feverishly stripping the region bare of beaver to discourage any American trappers from pushing farther north or west. The Snake watershed, including Jackson Hole, was part of the disputed Oregon country, which an 1818 treaty had opened to ten years' joint occupancy by the United States and Great Britain.[12] The British trappers felt that by leaving a strip of beaverless territory on the southwestern extremity of the Oregon country they could keep American trappers and settlers away from it and then in 1828 claim full title to it for Great Britain by virtue of America's failure to exercise her option of joint occupancy. Thanks to the efforts of Jedediah Smith and those who followed him, the British plan did not succeed. Jackson Hole and the rest of the Oregon country south of the Forty-ninth Parallel eventually became part of the United States.

Smith's route from Green River to the Snake, where he discovered the British, is a matter of conjecture. He could have traveled directly west toward Bear River (in present-day Idaho) and then north along the western edge of the Tetons, avoiding Jackson Hole altogether, as William H. Goetzmann[13] and Dale Morgan[14] believe. But in light of Smith's frustrated effort to visit Jackson Hole earlier that year (in February), it seems more probable that he ascended the Green, climbed the Hoback Rim, explored Jackson Hole, and then left the valley by either Conant or Teton Pass. A number of reliable historians[15] consider this theory more plausible.

After an informative sojourn at the Hudson's Bay post on Clark's Fork of the Columbia, Smith swung west and south of Jackson Hole and in the summer of 1825 arrived at Green River for the first annual rendezvous. Ashley distributed traps, guns, ammunition, and other "possibles" to his men, collected their furs, and returned with Smith to St. Louis, where he sold "the most valuable collection of furs ever bought" there.[16] In St. Louis, Smith became Ashley's partner, replacing Andrew Henry, who had come down from the mountains for good.[17]

Smith's and Ashley's route from the rendezvous to St. Louis took them to the Bighorn and then downstream to the Yellowstone and Missouri. At the Bighorn, twenty-five trappers accompanying them left the main body and turned west toward Jackson Hole, whose beaver resources may well have been a prime topic of conversation during the just-finished rendezvous as a result of Smith's spring visit there. The rather large group, which probably included Jim Bridger, Thomas Fitzpatrick, and David E. Jackson (after whom the valley was later named), ascended the Wind River and entered Jackson Hole over either Togwotee or Union Pass.[18]

Once in the valley, the trappers spread out along the streams in groups of two or three. They quietly paddled their canoes along the banks of the Snake, Buffalo, Gros Ventre, and Hoback rivers and their tributaries, making periodic stops to set traps or retrieve their catch. Most trapping and retrieving operations were performed at dusk or daybreak, when hostile Indians were least likely to be encountered. During the day, the men gathered in larger groups to skin the animals and stretch and dry their furs or to hunt fresh meat for the evening meal.

The typical beaver trap weighed about five pounds and had a long chain attached to one end. When the trapper found a likely spot for beaver, he waded into the shallow water, dug out a small flat area in the streambed and placed his trap there. The trap chain was attached to a piece of wood driven firmly into the ground. To attract a beaver to his set, the trapper rubbed a twig with castoreum (excretions collected from beaver sex glands) and hung it on a branch directly above the trap pan. A beaver would catch the scent, swim toward the twig, and upon reaching it trip the pan and catch his webbed foot in the trap's jaws. If the set worked well, the beaver would be pulled into deeper water and drowned before he could chew his leg free. In making a set, the trapper always had to be careful not to leave any human scent near by. He normally stayed in the water, but if he had to go ashore, the trapper always splashed water on the bank to cover his scent.[19]

In 1826, Ashley and Smith returned to the mountains for another rendezvous, held this time in present-day Cache Valley, Utah. After collecting furs from the Jackson Hole and other brigades, Ashley sold his firm to Jedediah Smith, David Jackson, and William L. Sublette, three of his most dependable employees, and returned to St. Louis with an abundance of furs, his financial fortune assured. Smith struck west for the Great Salt Lake desert country and the California settlements beyond to determine their fur-producing potential. Jackson, Sublette, and several brigades returned to the Upper Snake and eventually to Jackson Hole, where Jackson and others had had such a successful hunt the previous fall. The remaining brigades spread out over the Bear, Weber, and Green river systems south of Jackson Hole.[20]

The best evidence of a Smith-Jackson-Sublette brigade visiting Jackson Hole in the fall of 1826 is a letter written at the 1827 rendezvous by trapper Daniel Potts:

> We took a Northerly direction of about fifty miles, where we crossed Snake river, on the South fork of Columbia, at the forks of Henry's and Lewis's; at this place we were daily harassed by the Blackfeet: from thence we went up Henry's or North fork which bears North of East thirty miles and crossed a large rugged mountain [the Teton Range at either Conant or Teton Pass] which separates the two forks; from thence East up the other fork [through Jackson Hole] to its source, which heads on the top of the great chain of Rocky Mountains which separates the waters of the Atlantic from those of the Pacific.[21]

Potts went on to describe Yellowstone Lake and the nearby hot-spring basins.

For the next two years, Smith-Jackson-Sublette brigades combed the West, trapping the streams and memorizing the topography. Undoubtedly, several more trips were made to Jackson Hole. Jackson stayed in the mountains with the brigades and probably led some trappers into Jackson Hole at least once a year. Smith took a second and more costly trip overland to California to retrieve the men and furs he had left there on his previous excursion.[22] Sublette made periodic journeys to St. Louis for supplies, but always returned in time for rendezvous—held in 1827 and again in 1828 along the shores of Bear Lake on the present-day Idaho-Utah border.[23]

In Sublette's supply train heading west for the rendezvous of 1829 was an eighteen-year-old boy named Joseph Meek. According to Meek, Sublette led his troop into the Wind River Valley, up over either Togwotee or Union

Pass, and "fell in with Jackson in the valley of Lewis [Jackson] Lake, called Jackson's Hole, and remained on the borders of this lake for some time, waiting for Smith." While their men trapped in the shadows of the Tetons, Jackson and Sublette worried about Smith, who had not been seen since his second departure for California. Several search parties were dispatched.[24]

As they waited on the shores of Jackson Lake for the searchers to return, Sublette, according to local legend,[25] named the surrounding valley Jackson's Hole in honor of partner David E. Jackson, who had been trapping in the valley for years and who had completed another successful spring hunt there just before Sublette arrived. Despite the story, however, the place may have been named years before by some of Jackson's subordinates, to whom he was fondly known as Davey.[26] The exact time and place "Jackson's Hole" came into use will probably never be known, but 1837 saw its first appearance in a book.[27] The original Jackson's Hole has been shortened in recent years to Jackson Hole. It encompasses the region known to trappers as Jackson's Big Hole, the main valley, as well as Jackson's Little Hole, a small basin at the upper end of Hoback Canyon.

Word eventually got back to the men at Jackson Lake that Smith was west of the Tetons and heading east toward Pierre's Hole. Sublette and Jackson crossed the Tetons (probably at Conant Pass) and rendezvoused there with their long-lost partner. A combined force returned by way of Three Forks to Wind River for the winter. Losing his way on the return route, young Joe Meek stumbled upon the steaming geyser basins of Yellowstone Park, which reminded him of the mills at Pittsburgh. On April 1, 1830, as soon as the snow began melting off the passes, Jackson and

63

half the company headed west into Jackson Hole and the Snake country beyond.[28]

At the next rendezvous (1830), held near the confluence of the Popo Agie and Wind rivers, Smith, Jackson, and Sublette sold their firm to five employees, who subsequently formed a new enterprise, the Rocky Mountain Fur Company. Sublette agreed to continue supplying the firm at rendezvous time; Smith and Jackson returned to St. Louis, where they became involved in the growing Santa Fé trade. Smith was killed a year later in a Comanche ambush, and Jackson simply faded into oblivion, there being no recorded mention of him after March 20, 1833.[29]

What prompted the three men to sell out is not very clear. Beaver were not as plentiful as they once had been. The wilderness had been so thoroughly explored that not much was left for chronic adventurers like Smith, Jackson, and Sublette. The Blackfeet were as dangerous as ever, if not more so. Perhaps the decisive factor was the presence of a newly merged competitor backed by the Astor interests and known as the American Fur Company. Old John Jacob Astor had renewed his grandiose schemes for an empire in the West, and these were bound to come into conflict with the plans of trapping groups already in the field.

CHAPTER FIVE

FUR-TRADE RIVALRY AND DECLINE

The rivalry of the Rocky Mountain and American fur companies came to the fore in 1832, when several American Fur Company brigades appeared as uninvited guests at the Rocky Mountain Fur Company's rendezvous in Pierre's Hole. In reaching it, groups from both companies crossed Jackson Hole. One of the first to traverse the valley was William Sublette's supply train, accompanied by an inexperienced band of men under Nathaniel J. Wyeth of Cambridge, Massachusetts, who was making his debut in the fur trade. The Sublette-Wyeth party entered Jackson Hole by way of Hoback Canyon and on the Fourth of July, 1832, reached the banks of the Snake River, where, according to Wyeth's cousin, John B. Wyeth,

we drank the health of our friends in Massachusetts, in

good clear water, as that was the only liquor we had to drink in remembrance of our homes and dear connexions.[1]

Wyeth vividly described the difficult Snake ford:

... one man unloaded his horse, and swam across with him, leading two loaded ones, and unloading the two brought them back, for two more, and as Sublet's company and our own made over a hundred and fifty, we were all day in passing the river. In returning, my mule, by treading on a round stone, stumbled and threw me off, and the current was so strong, that a bush which I caught hold of only saved me from drowning.

The main body of the expedition ascended Teton Pass and waited at the summit for the stragglers, many of whom were too ill to walk. Nathaniel Wyeth had to cache supplies from several pack horses in order that sick men could ride. The physical strain of cross-country travel, combined with occasional shortages of food and water, had eroded the health and ambition of Wyeth's men, most of whom knew nothing of frontier life. Naturally, they found it more difficult to adopt the mountain men's mode of existence than did those who had been reared in the old frontier towns of the Ohio-Mississippi Basin.

After a meal of tree bark,[2] the Sublette-Wyeth party continued down into Pierre's Hole, where a large number of free trappers, engagés, and friendly Indians had assembled to trade furs for whisky, tobacco, rifles, knives, and other goods which Sublette had brought for them. Several brigades of American Fur Company men were also encamped, waiting for the arrival of their supply train. The free trappers, of which there was a growing number in the Rocky Mountains, were not connected with any outfit but nonetheless depended on the fur companies for supplies. Although they trapped where they wished and chose their associates, they always appeared at rendezvous to sell their furs to the highest bidder. The hired trappers, or engagés, who made up most of the company brigades, were paid according to a prearranged scale and given traps, horses, and other necessary items free of charge. The free trappers had to furnish their own equipment.

By 1832, the annual rendezvous was no longer the somber business engagement it had once been. Pierre's Hole was a scene of frivolity and emotional release rather than simply a place for the exchange of goods. After a year of hard work and constant exposure to danger, the trappers were eager to drink their fill of whisky, frolic with Indian maidens, bust out into a brawl, or gather around the campfires to spin their favorite yarns and guffaw at someone else's prevarications.

The gaiety of the rendezvous was interrupted by a band of hostile Gros Ventres returning from their annual visit with the Arapahoes. What followed became known in trapper lore as the Battle of Pierre's Hole. The whites and friendly Indians forced the Gros Ventres into a thicket, where the Gros Ventres dug a log-and-earth entrenchment. The hostiles successfully defended their fortress until evening and crept off in the dark. The exact number of Indians killed was never determined because the Gros Ventres dragged most of their dead away with them, but at least seven white trappers, twenty-five friendly Flatheads, and twenty-five horses were killed.[3]

After the battle, many of Nathaniel Wyeth's men concluded that the West was not for them and decided to return to Massachusetts at the earliest possible moment. One malcontent, George Moore, was so anxious to leave that he joined an unescorted group of six men heading for Teton Pass and Jackson Hole. What happened to Moore and his six comrades is best recorded in the diary of Warren A. Ferris, an American Fur Company employee who remained in Pierre's Hole:

> This evening [July 27, 1832] five of seven men who departed for St. Louis, three days since, returned, and informed us that they were attacked by a party of Indians in Jackson's Hole, and that two of their number, Moore and Fay [Foy], killed. The survivors saved themselves by flight, but one of them [Alfred Stevens] was wounded in the thigh.[4]

Stevens died of his wound and was buried in Pierre's Hole. The Indians who attacked the group were probably some of the same Gros Ventres who had participated in the Battle of Pierre's Hole.

The brigade to which Ferris was attached crossed Jackson Hole in early August and "saw the bones" of Moore and Foy. The men continued up the Hoback River to Jackson's Little Hole (Hoback Basin), where buffalo were plentiful and where remains of a recent Indian camp were discovered, and then crossed the Hoback into the Green River Valley, where they rendezvoused with American Fur Company suppliers. Afterward, a brigade under the command of Henry Vanderburgh and Andrew Drips hurried west into the Hoback Valley. According to Ferris, who accompanied the party,

> we halted for the night near the remains of two men [Moore and Foy], who were killed in July last. These we collected and deposited in a small stream, that discharged itself into a fork [Hoback] of Lewis [Snake] river; that flows from Jackson's Little Hole.[5]

The group crossed Jackson Hole and Teton Pass and fol-lowed the trail of a Rocky Mountain Fur Company brigade under Jim Bridger and Thomas Fitzpatrick. The American Fur Company people, who were not well acquainted with the area as yet, hoped that the Rocky Mountain outfit would lead them to the most productive beaver regions. But Bridger and Fitzpatrick anticipated the plan and led their rivals right through the heart of hostile Blackfoot country. The unsuspecting American Fur Company party was am-bushed and Vanderburgh brutally murdered, while the more experienced Rocky Mountain brigade was able to escape without a serious encounter.[6] Drips gave up the chase and returned to Jackson Hole by way of Pierre's Hole, then proceeded up Gros Ventre Canyon and down to Green River via Union Pass.[7]

By the summer of 1833, competition between the Rocky Mountain and American Fur companies was so intense that each company faced financial disaster. Contracts with sup-pliers who had affiliations with rivals were broken; Indians were encouraged by each company to rob the other firm's brigades; dishonor and treachery went far beyond the decep-tion and trickery which had caused Vanderburgh's death. At a joint rendezvous in 1833, the two companies called a truce and divided the beaver country so that each could trap in peace.

The American Fur Company obtained rights to the land west of the Continental Divide and immediately sent an expedition under Robert Newell and Warren Ferris north-west through Jackson Hole to the Flatheads on the Colum-bia. It returned via Jackson Hole and the Hoback the following spring. The Rocky Mountain Fur Company acquired the land east of the Continental Divide.[8] A year later, however, the company was disintegrating and in 1836 was dissolved.

About the same time, John Jacob Astor sold his interests in the American Fur Company's Western Department to the St. Louis firm of Pratte, Chouteau and Company. A substantial segment of the market for beaver pelts would soon disappear, he predicted, noting that London style had switched from fur hats to silk and that this was bound to have a very detrimental effect on the demand for beaver pelts from the Rocky Mountains. Astor's analysis proved to be correct, for in only a few short years the great Rocky Mountain fur trade came to a standstill, largely because of the change in European fashions.[9]

A new era in the history of the West was beginning. It was marked by the appearance in Jackson Hole of the Reverend Samuel Parker, a missionary sent west to Christianize the Indians of the Oregon country.[10]

Parker entered Jackson Hole over the Hoback Rim after camping at Green River during the rendezvous of 1835. With him were a brigade of trappers, including Kit Carson and Jim Bridger, and a band of Nez Percés and Flatheads who had been enthralled by Parker's religious teachings and had decided to lead him to their homeland. On Sunday, August 23, 1835, while the expedition was camped in Hoback Basin, Parker conducted the first Christian worship service in the Rocky Mountains. His journal reveals what transpired:

> In the afternoon we had public worship with those of the company who understood English. The men conducted with great propriety, and listened with attention. I did not feel any disposition to upbraid them for their sins, but endeavored affectionately to show them, that they were unfit for heaven, and that they could not be happy in the employments of that holy place, unless they should first experience a great moral change of

heart by the grace of God, since the only source of
happiness in heaven consists in serving and glorifying
God forever. The place of our encampment was such
as would naturally fill the mind with solemnity . . . .[11]

Upon reaching the main part of Jackson Hole, Bridger
sent "several of his men into the mountains to hunt and
trap." As "they rode away," Parker prayed "for their safety
and salvation."[12]

One day an Indian led Parker to a high place in the
southern end of Jackson Hole where the missionary looked
out onto "a scene of perfect enchantment":

Not very far to the north, the Trois Tetons . . . were
distinctly visible, with two others of the same form but
of less magnitude. Only three of the cluster are so
high as to be seen at a very *great* distance. Here I spent
much time in looking over the widely extended and
varied scenery, sometimes filled with emotions of the
sublime, in beholding the towering mountains; sometimes with pleasure in tracing the windings of the
streams in the vale below; and these sensations frequently gave place to astonishment in viewing the
courses in which the rivers flow on their way un-
obstructed by mountain barriers. After some hours
occupied in this excursion, I descended to the encampment much gratified with what I had seen of the works
of God.[13]

When the party attempted to ascend Teton Pass, it encountered a stampede of buffalo coming straight toward it.
Parker's journal reveals that one buffalo "ran over a horse on
the back of which was a child, . . . but providentially it was
not injured."[14] After witnessing this hair-raising spectacle,
the caravan proceeded into Pierre's Hole, where Parker took
leave of the white men and headed cross country with his

Nez Percé bodyguards toward their home on the Salmon River. He did not last long in the West. Becoming despondent over his health and the limited accomplishments of his mission, he set sail for New London, Connecticut, in June, 1836.[15] His experience, however, established a precedent for later missionaries and settlers.

In 1836, a band of American Fur Company trappers under Osborne Russell entered Jackson Hole through Gros Ventre Canyon and proceeded north to Jackson Lake, which Russell complained was "infested with innumerable swarms of horse flies and musketoes."[16] The party ascended Pacific Creek to Two Ocean Pass and descended into the Yellowstone country, where it met another party under Jim Bridger.[17] The combined forces returned to Green River via Jackson Hole and Gros Ventre Canyon in the spring of 1837.[18] Russell and a small brigade re-entered Yellowstone in the fall via Hoback River, Jackson Hole, and Two Ocean Pass.[19] Russell spent considerable time in Jackson Hole the next few years, despite the fact that the region was yielding fewer and fewer beaver. At the 1838 rendezvous on the Popo Agie, a rumor spread "among the men that the company intended to bring no more supplies to the Rocky Mountains and discontinue all further operations." With this distressing thought in mind, he entered Jackson Hole that fall by way of Gros Ventre Canyon and encountered about sixty men under Andrew Drips and Jim Bridger. Part of Russell's time in the valley was spent trapping along Spread Creek. The trappers left Jackson Hole over Teton Pass and trapped along the western slope of the Tetons.[20] One American Fur Company brigade, which included Robert Newell, spent Christmas Day, 1838, in Jackson Hole.[21]

In 1839, Russell returned to Jackson Hole for his last visit and camped along the shore of Jackson Lake in early July. Later, he journeyed north to Yellowstone Lake, where he and his partner were ambushed by some Indians and forced to escape across the extreme northern end of Jackson Hole and through Conant Pass.[22]

Following the lead of Samuel Parker, Pierre-Jean De Smet, a Belgian Jesuit priest, passed through Jackson Hole in 1840 on his way to the Flathead Indian villages, where he planned to investigate prospects for a Catholic mission. Father De Smet, a deputation of Flatheads, and ten Canadian trappers entered Jackson Hole through Hoback Canyon and descended to the banks of the Snake River. De Smet noted that to get him across the raging torrent the Flatheads

> made a kind of sack of my skin tent; then they put all my things in and set me on top of it. The three Flatheads who had jumped in to guide my frail bark by swimming, told me, laughing not to be afraid, that I was on an excellent boat. And in fact this machine floated on the water like a majestic swan; and in less than ten minutes I found myself on the other bank, where we encamped for the night.[23]

With De Smet's passage through Jackson Hole, the great fur-trade era in the American West came to an end. No more rendezvous were held after 1840, although a few small groups of trappers remained in the mountains. With the decline in world demand for beaver pelts and the growing scarcity of beaver, no St. Louis or New York company was willing to finance a supply train to the Rocky Mountains. The more ambitious of the mountain men turned to new horizons and new opportunities. So it was that men like Bridger, Newell, Meek, and Fitzpatrick guided the first pioneers over the Oregon Trail.

73

The age of exploration and exploitation had ended, and the age of settlement was beginning. Jackson Hole, which for thirty years had been the crossroads of the Rocky Mountains, returned for a time to its primeval solitude. Meanwhile, long wagon trains of emigrants, profiting from the mountain men's topographical discoveries, crossed the Rockies over an easier route many miles to the south.

Part II   **SURVEY AND SETTLEMENT**

CHAPTER SIX

RAILROAD SURVEYS AND THE RAYNOLDS EXPEDITION

The first wagonloads of settlers bound for the fertile farm-lands of Oregon and California invariably crossed the Rocky Mountains over a low ridge on the Wind River Range, lying southeast of Jackson Hole, known as South Pass.[1] It provided the least difficult tramontane wagon route of any point along the North American continent's rugged and protruding spine. Had a ridge as easy for wagons to cross as South Pass not existed, the history of Jackson Hole after 1840 would have been vastly different from what it actually was; for without South Pass, Jackson Hole would have offered the most accessible and best-explored route through the north-central Rockies. Although the Togwotee and Union Pass entrances on the east rim of the valley were more difficult to negotiate than South Pass, the westward-pressing pioneers would have had no alternative but to travel

77

over one or the other of those routes through Jackson Hole.

In fact, such paths of migration had been suggested. In 1811, John Colter had mentioned to Henry Brackenridge the possibility of taking wagons over what must have been Togwotee Pass.[2] And in 1839, just two years before the first substantial caravan of settlers crossed South Pass, Captain Washington Hood of the U.S. Army's Topographical Engineers had devised "a practicable route for wheeled vehicles across the mountains" by way of Jackson Hole. Hood had suggested that pioneers could ascend Green River

> toward its headwaters, as far as Horse creek, one of its tributaries, follow out this last mentioned stream to its source by a westerly course, across the main ridge [Hoback Rim] in order to attain Jackson's Little Hole, at the headwaters of Jackson's fork [Hoback River]. Follow down Jackson's fork to its mouth and decline to the northward along Lewis's fork [Snake River], passing through Jackson's Big Hole to about twelve miles beyond Yellowstone [?] pass, crossing on the route a nameless beaver stream. Here the route passes due west over another prong of the ridge [Teton Pass?], a fraction worse than the former, followed until it has attained the headwaters of Pierre's Hole . . . .[3]

If either Colter's or Hood's suggested route had been adopted as the main thoroughfare for westward migration, Jackson Hole would have been settled long before the 1880's. A military post probably would have been built in the valley to protect passing wagon trains from marauding Blackfeet, and some travel-weary emigrants undoubtedly would have settled around the post. Civilization would have come to Jackson Hole much as it came to many strategic points along the actual Overland Trail. Conceivably, the valley would have been linked to the transcontinental railroad and would have prospered greatly as a result.

Because of geographic circumstances, however, neither Colter's nor Hood's route was adopted, for an easier route—South Pass—*did* exist and countless trains of emigrants *were* able to avoid the higher passes and rugged canyon entrances into Jackson Hole. And Jackson Hole was able to avoid the curses and blessings of civilization for at least another generation.

During the 1840's and 1850's, a few solitary trappers and the usual number of Indian hunting parties wandered through the valley, but aside from their infrequent visits, Jackson Hole remained relatively unoccupied until 1860. Meanwhile, the rest of the country moved rapidly ahead. The first pioneers over South Pass flocked to the lush Willamette, San Joaquin, and Sacramento valleys in the Far West. In 1847, Brigham Young's dispossessed Mormons established their desert kingdom along the Great Salt Lake, southwest of Jackson Hole. In the Northwest, the boundary dispute with Great Britain was finally resolved by the treaty of June, 1846. South of the Forty-ninth Parallel, the Oregon country, including Jackson Hole, became exclusive property of the United States, thereby terminating the joint Anglo-American occupancy in effect since 1818. And in the Southwest, the annexation of Texas (1845) precipitated the Mexican War and the eventual acquisition of Mexico's vast northern possessions, including California. Adding California was a crucial event, for the discovery of gold there in 1848 quickly multiplied by a hundredfold the hordes of adventurous Americans moving west.[4]

The new but uncharted territories and the growing number of people seeking new lives there created grave problems and responsibilities for the government at Washington.

Foremost among them was the protection of settlers and gold seekers from hostile Indians. In order to furnish it, the army built military posts at strategic points throughout the West and dispatched reconnaissance patrols to map the Indians' land and to estimate the military strength and intentions of the various tribes. In a conscious effort to promote emigration, the army also conducted surveys for potential roads and railroads.[5]

In 1853, Congress authorized the Department of War to survey all possible transcontinental railroad routes. Secretary of War Jefferson Davis sent four official parties into the field: one across the continent along the forty-seventh and forty-ninth parallels north of Jackson Hole and the other three along the thirty-eighth, thirty-fifth, and thirty-second parallels far to the south of the valley. The legislature of newly organized Washington Territory dispatched an expedition under Frederick West Lander to determine a possible railroad route from Puget Sound diagonally southeast to South Pass. The Lander party examined the mountainous regions immediately south of Jackson Hole and thus became the first major railroad survey group to pass close to it.[6]

The results of the Pacific Railroad Surveys, as they are called, were not conclusive. Each field party defended its own line of survey as the best possible route. Southern congressmen and Secretary Davis were partial to a route along the Thirty-second Parallel, whereas northern congressmen were uniformly opposed to any route, especially the Thirty-second, that would place the railroad's eastern terminus (with all the economic advantages such a terminus implied) in the South. Because of these sectional implications, the railroad controversy could not be resolved in a Congress already badly split over the tariff and slavery issues. Only

Jackson Hole from Peak 10552, southeast of Static Peak

Remains of a corral possibly used by horse thieves making their escape
through Flat Creek Canyon

View from Snake River Overlook, Dead Man's Bar at lower right

The Tetons from Taggart Creek

Hidden Falls,
west of Jenny Lake

A cabin used in the motion picture *Shane*

Leigh and Jackson lakes from Indian Paintbrush Canyon

The first schoolhouse, South Park

"Wilderness Acres," the John Dodge homestead near Wilson

Cathedral Group from near String Lake

The Tetons reflected in the Blacktail Ponds

Diorama of Rendezvous at Pierre's Hole (1832)

Lake Solitude from Paintbrush Divide

The Tetons from the Joe Pfeiffer homestead, Mormon Row

the secession of the South would make possible a final decision on the transcontinental railroad.[7]

In the intervening years before the South seceded, the War Department managed to send several additional railroad reconnaissance expeditions into the West. One of them, commanded by Captain William F. Raynolds of the Topographical Engineers and guided by old Jim Bridger, entered Jackson Hole in the summer of 1860, thereby focusing the attention of the civilized world upon the valley for the first time in nearly twenty years. Raynolds had been ordered to explore the regions about the Upper Yellowstone, Gallatin, and Madison rivers and

> to ascertain . . . the numbers, habits and disposition of the Indians inhabiting the country, its agricultural and mineralogical resources, its climate and . . . streams, its topographical features, and the facilities or obstacles . . . to the construction of rail or common roads, either to meet the wants of military operations or those of emigration through, or settlement in, the country.[8]

Raynolds did not originally intend to cross the Continental Divide into Jackson Hole, but upon reaching the headwaters of the Wind River, he was advised that a direct route from the Wind to the source of the Yellowstone was blocked by an impassable basaltic ridge. Using traditional mountain man hyperbole, guide Jim Bridger triumphantly informed him: "I told you you could not go through. A bird can't fly over that without taking a supply of grub along."[9] Turning west, Bridger led the expedition over Union Pass (named by Raynolds) to the upper waters of the Gros Ventre. Several times Bridger tried to find a pass north through the Mount Leidy Highlands toward Togwotee and

97

Two Ocean passes but was unsuccessful because of deep snows and his own failing memory. (According to Raynolds, Bridger had not visited the region for at least fifteen years.) Giving up any hope of reaching the headwaters of the Yellowstone, Raynolds and company continued down the Gros Ventre and on June 10, 1860, crossed to its south bank a short distance above the Gros Ventre's junction with the Snake River in Jackson Hole.[10]

Bridger declared there was no ford upstream on the Snake and advised the expedition to push downstream along the east bank. Raynolds journeyed upstream for eight miles before concluding that Bridger was not mistaken. It is not evident in Raynolds' journal why the party failed to consider a possible line of travel north through Jackson Hole along the east bank of the Snake, across Buffalo River, up Pacific Creek to Two Ocean Pass, and down into the Upper Yellowstone—the very area Raynolds desired above all else to explore. Perhaps Bridger deemed the snow in the Yellowstone Highlands too deep and never mentioned this possible northward route to Raynolds. More likely, however, the Old Man of the Mountains had forgotten those trapper trails through the upper reaches of Jackson Hole which he had explored in the late 1830's. In any case, Raynolds' men moved down the Snake in search of a ford. En route, they spotted a party of Blackfeet along the Gros Ventre foothills and later met a friendly band of Snakes (Shoshonis) swimming their horses across the river from the Teton side.[11]

At the site of the Indians' ford, Lance Corporal Bradley attempted a crossing and was drowned in the snowmelt-swollen waters. Fearing a repetition of Bradley's accident, Raynolds moved his company farther downstream to an easier ford and there constructed a raft, which, when tested, "behaved so badly that it was promptly pronounced a complete failure." Meanwhile, the more wilderness-wise Bridger constructed a boat, using a framework of cottonwood saplings bound together with leather thongs and covered with resin-coated animal skins. It carried all the expedition's supplies and equipment across the river except the odometers which slipped from a raft in midstream and were never recovered.

On June 18, while the caravan was crossing Teton Pass into Pierrc's Hole, Raynolds noticed a pine tree bearing an inscription, perhaps carved by trapper Joe Meek: "J. M., July 7th, 1832" and "July 11, 1833." The expedition pushed north toward Henry's Lake and the Upper Missouri the following day.[12]

In his report to the secretary of war, Raynolds discouraged the idea of rail transportation across the Continental Divide to Jackson Hole and the Yellowstone, asserting that the "summit of the ridge is lofty throughout, and I do not believe it will ever be thought expedient to cross it by rail."[13] By making such a statement, Raynolds unwittingly contributed to the efforts of later conservationists to protect the beauties of Jackson Hole and the wilderness areas north of the valley from those uglifying tendencies of civilization which inevitably accompany the appearance of an iron horse.

CHAPTER SEVEN

GOLD FEVER

Not long after Raynolds returned east to fight in the Civil War, another expedition of an entirely different nature approached the valley through Snake River Canyon. It consisted of forty-two miners fresh from the Montana gold camps, a hundred airline miles northwest of Jackson Hole. According to Walter W. De Lacy, their elected leader, some of the men were "bad characters," and at least one was subsequently executed by a band of vigilantes. The miners had come from Virginia City, Montana Territory, the site of the most recent post-California gold strike.[1] The replacement of placer mining in California's gold fields by the more expensive deep-rock and hydraulic methods had forced many small-time stream prospectors (like those in the De Lacy group) to move east or northeast of California into regions where stream deposits might still be discovered.

The luckier ones staked claims along rich placers in present-day Colorado, Nevada (the Comstock Lode), and Idaho. Then, in 1863, the miners stampeded to a strike at Alder Gulch in Montana, where Virginia City quickly sprang up.[2]

De Lacy and his compatriots entering Jackson Hole in the summer of 1863 reached Virginia City after the best areas had been thoroughly staked. They resolved instead to prospect along the south branch of the Snake, a promising area not yet visited by the multiplying hordes of gold seekers. At the lower end of Jackson Hole, they panned the waters of the Hoback and Gros Ventre; finding no gold, they continued up the valley. Upon reaching Pacific Creek,[3] near the outlet of Jackson Lake, they erected a corral and held a meeting, governed, surprisingly enough, by the rules of parliamentary procedure. During the session, which was itself a simple yet highly meaningful demonstration of frontier democracy, the miners adopted two regulations giving group sanction to the protection of individual rights. The regulations, as De Lacy later recalled them, were:

1. That every person present should be regarded as a discoverer, in each and every gulch found by any party or member of a party.
2. That each member, as discoverer, should be entitled to five claims of two hundred feet each along the gulch viz., a discovery claim, and a pre-emption claim in the main gulch, a bar claim, a hill claim, and a patch claim.[4]

From August 28 to 31, 1861, two teams of prospectors laboriously panned Pacific Creek and its neighboring streams, but to no avail. After a third team assigned to explore Buffalo River (and possibly Black Rock Creek) returned to camp with no news of gold, the restless miners split into two groups, one under De Lacy heading north into the Yellowstone geyser basins and the other backtracking through Jackson Hole and Snake River Canyon.[5] They found nothing in the valley, but this did not discourage future mining ventures there. In fact, the very next year, a second party of Montana miners led by George H. Phelps traversed the region.[6] Nor would the first settlers of Jackson Hole be immune to De Lacy's type of gold fever in later years.

CHAPTER EIGHT

ARMY EXPLORATION AND HAYDEN'S SURVEYS

In Montana, De Lacy's stories about geysers and other thermal phenomena in the Yellowstone area generated considerable curiosity, especially among the more prominent citizens. In 1870, several of them, under the leadership of Henry D. Washburn, territorial surveyor-general, were escorted by Lieutenant Gustavus C. Doane and a small cavalry detachment into the Yellowstone country to verify De Lacy's findings.[1] The Washburn-Doane expedition was followed in 1871 by two official government exploring parties, one acting under the sanction of the War Department and the other under orders from the Interior Department. These simultaneous explorations marked the beginning of a bitter and rather wasteful bureaucratic rivalry. For the next eight years, each department duplicated the work of the other as each hastened to become the first

103

government agency to complete a survey of all the territories. The War Department party was led by Captain J. W. Barlow of the Corps of Engineers.[2] At the head of the Interior Department group was Professor Ferdinand Vandiveer Hayden, veteran of the Raynolds expedition and founder of the United States Geological Survey of the Territories.[3] Despite the rivalry of their superiors in Washington, Barlow and Hayden were able to co-operate to some extent in the field. The chief result of their work was the first nationwide publicity concerning the Yellowstone region and its subsequent designation as a national park.

In 1872, Hayden returned to the West, this time with two survey divisions, one under his assistant, James Stevenson, and the other under Hayden's own direction. Hayden led the Yellowstone Division south from Fort Ellis, Montana, into the newly established national park, while Stevenson directed the Snake River Division north from the Union Pacific station at Ogden, Utah, to Pierre's Hole on the western side of the Tetons. Stevenson intended to rendezvous with Hayden in Yellowstone later that year.[4]

In Stevenson's company were Nathaniel P. Langford, first superintendent of Yellowstone Park, and William Henry Jackson, the photographer whose beautiful plates from the 1871 Hayden expedition had been instrumental in persuading Congress to create America's first national park. Professor Frank H. Bradley served Stevenson as chief geologist, and W. R. Taggart was Bradley's assistant. Head topographer was Gustavus R. Bechler. Among the other assistants whom Hayden had assigned to Stevenson's party were two young men destined for renown in the scientific and cultural worlds: botanist John Merle Coulter and ornithologist C. Hart Merriam.

After working with the Hayden surveys, Coulter moved

on to establish an academic reputation in botany and was later president of two middle western institutions of higher education, Indiana State University and Lake Forest College. Merriam founded the United States Biological Survey and served as a trustee of the National Geographic Society. Henry Gannett, a young Harvard-educated geographer with Hayden's Yellowstone Division, became chief geographer for the United States Geological Survey (created in 1879) and was a founder and early president of the National Geographic Society. Another youthful member of the Yellowstone Division, W. H. Holmes, used the reputation he had built for himself as Hayden's landscape artist-topographer to become director of the National Collection of Fine Arts.[5]

In Pierre's Hole, Stevenson and his talented staff retained the services of Richard "Beaver Dick" Leigh as guide. An Englishman who had run away to sea as a child and later became involved in the American fur trade, Leigh lived like a latter-day mountain man in a crude tipi with his Shoshoni wife, Jenny, and their children. Leigh was especially familiar with the Jackson Hole–Teton Mountains–Pierre's Hole region. Because Stevenson's party wished to examine the Tetons at closer range, Leigh guided them up Teton Creek on the west slope of the mountains. Upon reaching the higher elevations, five men from the expedition attempted to climb the Grand Teton, and of these, two—Stevenson and Langford—claimed to have reached the summit.

The claim went undisputed until 1898, when William Owen, Frank Petersen, Franklin Spalding, and John Shive climbed the Grand Teton and discovered that Langford's published description of the summit did not match what they saw.[6] Owen published his group's claim of first ascent, and a bitter controversy soon raged. Langford reiterated his original story, while Owen retorted that no evidence of the Langford party's presence could be found on the summit. Photographer W. H. Jackson, loyal to his 1872 compatriots, thought Owen was not very realistic in expecting to find evidence of a climb made twenty-six years earlier.[7] But mountain climbers normally mark their successes by erecting piles of rocks known as cairns. It is likely that Langford and Stevenson would have erected a cairn had they reached the top, and it is unlikely that the stone structure would have been totally obliterated in twenty-six years. At any rate, Owen accumulated considerable political influence and in 1929 got the Wyoming Legislature to award the distinction of first ascent to his party. A plaque in their honor now rests atop the Grand Teton.[8]

While Stevenson, Langford, and company were climbing the Grand Teton, W. H. Jackson was perched on a ridge two canyons to the west of them busily recording the fantastic mountain scenery on his photographic plates. Risking life and limb as he crawled out along the rocky precipices of Table Mountain, he managed to get several excellent shots of the Tetons, the first photographs ever taken of those historic trappers' landmarks. Because photographic technique was still in its infancy, he took all of his cumbersome developing equipment along the precipice with him. Old Molly, the mule who carried his tripod, plates, cameras, dark box, chemicals, and water for washing the plates, was a highly valued member of the survey team. If she were to stumble over the brink, most of the equipment would be dashed to pieces with her on the rocks below. Loss of equipment could threaten the continuation of Hayden's surveys, for Jackson's pictures were the most effective means of publicizing the expedition's accomplishments. Without such publicity,

Hayden might have been unable to secure federal appropriations to continue his work, especially since he sometimes obtained support by presenting Washington's lawmakers with gift folios of Jackson's photographs.[9]

Knowing the importance of Old Molly to the continuation of Hayden's civilian surveys (and Jackson's own employment as well), Jackson took special precautions when leading her along the precarious ledges which he was wont to explore. Even so, she and her valued equipment were often in danger. Jackson later recalled an occasion on which he was trying to get a close-up view of the Grand Teton:

> On one side was a sheer precipice, but on the other a ledge supported a bank of hard snow which offered a passage around the wall. The snow, however, lay at a dangerously steep angle and overhung a drop of several hundred feet. It was with some misgivings that we contemplated this passage. Snow is treacherous. If one of the animals should happen to strike a soft spot and fall on that steep incline, there was a possibility of going over into the chasm below. However, as this was the only way to get a close-up view of the magnificent peaks, we decided to take the risk. As a precaution, we first prepared a way by tramping out a trail and then leading over the saddle animals. Finally we followed with Old Molly and her precious pack, relying upon a firm hold on the halter strap to keep her from falling over the cliff if any mishap should occur. Fortunately none did.[10]

After an all too brief geologic-photographic examination of the Teton Range, the Snake River Division moved north along the western base of the Tetons to Madison River and Yellowstone Park. Stevenson had originally intended to cross over Teton Pass into Jackson Hole with the main part of his caravan while sending a smaller party to explore a secondary route through Snake River Canyon, but Beaver Dick Leigh told Stevenson that the latter route was too dangerous. In mid-September, after replenishing its supplies at the Yellowstone rendezvous, the Snake River Division turned south and approached Jackson Hole along the Upper Snake. Near Conant Pass Trail, the surveyors were reunited with Leigh, who had crossed the mountains since they last saw him in Pierre's Hole.

In Jackson Hole the Snake River Division conducted an extensive geological and topographical survey. One party explored the east shore of Jackson Lake and conducted depth soundings farther out. Another group traveled up the Buffalo River. The main part of the expedition made camps at the inlet and subsequently at the outlet of Jackson Lake, then along String Lake, then near present-day Moose, and finally at the base of Teton Pass. Most of the company then proceeded over Teton Pass, while a small party negotiated the supposedly treacherous Snake River Canyon exit. Geologist Bradley, who accompanied the latter group, was amazed to discover that the canyon "really presents but very slight obstacles to building a railroad, if one were desired from this point to Yellowstone Lake or . . . to the rich basins of Jackson's Hole."[11]

Many of the more spectacular topographical features in Jackson Hole were named for members of Hayden's 1872 survey team. Mount Moran was named for Thomas Moran, an artist for the Yellowstone Division who never actually visited the valley, and Mount Leidy was named for Joseph Leidy, Hayden's paleontologist. The five jewel-like lakes at the eastern base of the Tetons commemorate guide Beaver Dick Leigh and his wife, Jenny; geologist Frank H. Bradley and his assistant, W. R. Taggart; and George H. Phelps, "a hunter of the region" who had panned for gold there in 1864. Hayden's men coined some other names, but they never became popular; for example, Mount Hayden for the Grand Teton, North Gros Ventre Butte for Blacktail Butte, and East Teton River for Cottonwood Creek.[12]

In 1877, the Hayden survey's Teton Division, led by Gustavus R. Bechler, returned to Wyoming to map considerable portions of Jackson Hole.[13] A year later, Frederick C. Clark's Wind River Division mapped the rest of the valley.[14] The chief geologist on both expeditions was Orestes St. John, for whom one of the Teton peaks north of Cascade Canyon was named. A photographic party under William Henry Jackson also went through the valley in 1878 en route to the Yellowstone. Jackson took several photographs of the Tetons from Signal Mountain, but "because of a smoky haziness [caused by forest fires in the vicinity] that filled the air," they were not satisfactory.[15] W. H. Holmes, who was with Jackson, made several beautiful sketches of the Tetons and Jackson Hole which were made into plates for Hayden's annual report.[16]

During the peak Hayden years, army surveyors also visited Jackson Hole. Captain William A. Jones's reconnaissance in 1873 accomplished what Captain Raynolds had failed to do in 1860: locate a direct route for a military road from Wind River to Yellowstone River.[17] On a return trip from Yellowstone Park by way of Two Ocean Pass, Lava Creek, and Black Rock Creek in Jackson Hole, Jones rediscovered the long-forgotten Togwotee Pass. Fortunately, his recommendation to build a road over this pass and north to Two Ocean Pass was never approved by Congress. Today the region that Jones's road would have traversed is one of the more beautiful wilderness areas in the world, one in which no motorized vehicles of any sort are permitted.

Jones's reconnaissance mission was followed three years later by the most poorly timed and ill-conceived military expedition ever to visit Jackson Hole. Under orders "to make an exploration of Snake River from Yellowstone Lake to Columbia River" in the dead of winter, Lieutenant Gustavus C. Doane and six cavalrymen left Fort Ellis, Montana Territory, on October 11, 1876. After struggling through snow and sleet in Yellowstone Park, they arrived at the head of Jackson Lake on November 23. Rather unwisely, Doane chose to lead his men around the west shore of the lake, where fallen timber and glacial runoff made horse travel and even human travel almost impossible. The men took seven days to cover a mere thirty-two miles. As they moved around the lake, three men had to remain offshore in a boat while the other four guided the stock around wind-fallen trees along the shore. By the time they began their descent of the river at the outlet of Jackson Lake, the men had consumed nearly all their rations. Had it not been for the fishing skill of Private Warren and the generosity of John Pierce, a trapper spending the winter in a cabin at the south end of the valley, Doane and his men would surely have starved to death. While they did survive the trip through Jackson Hole, they nearly perished again on their way out of the valley. Passing down the Snake River Canyon, they lost their boat and most of their supplies, and were reduced to a diet of horse meat for the duration of the journey to Fort Hall, Idaho Territory. There, Doane began to build a new boat and to gather additional supplies for the continuation of his expedition, but he was ordered back to Fort Ellis before the boat was completed.[18]

Doane's journey through Jackson Hole and Snake River Canyon typified the foolhardy nature of much army exploration during the 1860's and 1870's. (The attempt by members of Hayden's civilian survey to climb the Grand Teton without proper equipment, however, was nearly as foolish a venture.) Why the expedition was undertaken is not known, but if the army had needed an accurate survey of the Snake River region, it certainly could have waited until spring. Whatever may have been the reasoning behind it, the mission very nearly cost the lives of seven men.

Both the Doane and the Jones expeditions demonstrated the inability of army surveyors to compete successfully with their civilian counterparts in the exploration of western lands. In terms of preparation, manpower, and field technology, Hayden's surveys in Jackson Hole were superior to those of Lieutenant Doane and Captain Jones. But it is unfair to generalize about army exploration solely on the basis of Doane's and Jones's experiences. In other areas of the West, the army conducted surveys—notably Lieutenant George M. Wheeler's—which were better manned and more soundly conceived and which produced far more substantial results. But even Lieutenant Wheeler's "Geographical Surveys of the Territories of the United States West of the 100th Meridian" were inferior to Professor Hayden's in the extent of their scientific sophistication and, perhaps more important, in the effectiveness of their publicity.

In an age when pragmatism was just coming into its own, Ferdinand Vandiveer Hayden, unlike many of his less imaginative military counterparts, had already grasped the importance of publicity in guaranteeing the success of a scientific endeavor. His philosophy was based on one vital consideration: the continuation of his work was entirely dependent upon the willingness of Congress to grant him annual appropriations. To assure congressional favor, he catered not only to the personal whims of influential congressmen but also to the interests of the powerful lobbyists who stood behind them. Hayden sought and obtained the support of many leading eastern scientists and university professors who, once they realized their own stake in the preservation of nonmilitary exploration, gladly testified before Congress in favor of civilian surveys like Hayden's. They recognized that organized science prospered best in an environment free from the typically military considerations of expediency and secrecy. They also understood that military discipline ran counter to the traditions of intellectual freedom, of which they, as academicians, were most proud.

Hayden geared his work to both the academic interests of science and the pecuniary desires of business and commerce. In subject and language, his annual reports were designed to attract the favorable attention of capitalists interested in promoting western development. But more important than the help from either business or science was the support Hayden elicited from the general public. Through wide distribution of Jackson's spectacular wet-plate photographs, Moran's glowing canvases, and Holmes's unique panoramas, he dramatized the beauty of the land he had surveyed and established for his explorations a reputation which surpassed those of all others, both military and civilian. It enhanced the popularity of civilian surveys in general and led, in 1879, to the elimination of military surveys in the West and the creation of a civilian bureau, the United States Geological Survey, to co-ordinate government exploration. Thanks to the efforts of Hayden and others like him, the American tradition of civilian supremacy over the military was reinforced.[19]

CHAPTER NINE

PRESIDENT ARTHUR GOES FISHING

During the 1880's and 1890's, as the first permanent settlers were arriving in Jackson Hole, additional government and private expeditions visited the valley. In 1881, Major Julius W. Mason escorted John Wesley Hoyt, territorial governor of Wyoming, through Jackson Hole along the approximate Two Ocean–Togwotee Pass route taken by Captain Jones in 1873. Like Jones, Hoyt was looking for a practical wagon route into Yellowstone Park from the southwest.[1]

A year later, Lieutenant General Philip H. Sheridan, commander of the Military Division of the Missouri, toured the Jackson Hole region as part of his annual reconnaissance through potentially hostile Indian country.[2] Ever since Custer's massacre at the Little Bighorn in 1876, the American military establishment had been maintaining a very close surveillance of the Indians in order to predict and at-

113

tempt to prevent future uprisings. Sheridan's company entered Jackson Hole over a low area between Togwotee and Union passes which Sheridan named Robert Lincoln Pass[3] in honor of Secretary of War Robert T. Lincoln, who had originally intended to travel with him. U.S. Inspector General D. B. Sacket, who accompanied the expedition, reported that "rich placer gold mines have been discovered and are being worked in the Teton Basin [Jackson Hole], on the Gros Ventre and on the Buffalo Fork of Snake River."[4] His statement confirms the fact that prospectors were panning the streams of Jackson Hole during the early 1880's. It is doubtful, however, that the mines were as rich as Sacket said they were, for no other writers have corroborated his estimate. His enthusiasm for the natural beauty of the valley apparently carried over into an exaggerated estimate of its mineral wealth, for no significant deposits have ever been discovered in Jackson Hole.

General Sheridan returned to the valley in 1883, this time with a distinguished party. Accompanying him were President Chester A. Arthur, Secretary of War Lincoln (considered a likely presidential candidate in 1884), Missouri Senator George G. Vest, Montana Territorial Governor John Schuyler Crosby, and a host of lesser dignitaries. Also present were photographer F. Jay Haynes, chief packer Tom Moore and his assistants, some Indian guides, and an armed escort of seventy-five cavalrymen under the command of Captain E. M. Hayes. President Arthur had come west with Sheridan for three reasons: to relax, to acquaint himself with western geography, and to learn more about the American Indian.

After a meeting with Washakie, venerable chief of the Shoshonis, at the Wind River Reservation east of Jackson Hole, the presidential caravan crossed the Continental

Divide at Robert Lincoln Pass and descended into Gros Ventre Canyon, where President Arthur discovered some excellent trout fishing. The expedition made five temporary camps in the Jackson Hole area: Camp Isham and Camp Arthur, along Gros Ventre River; Camp Teton, three and a half miles southwest of Blacktail Butte; Camp Hampton, ten miles east of Leigh Lake; and Camp Strong, on the Snake River above Jackson Lake.

Even in the wilderness the President was in contact with the outside world, thanks to the efforts of mounted military couriers operating out of Fort Ellis, Montana Territory, and Fort Washakie, Wyoming Territory. Press coverage of the trip was scanty, however, and often contrived. Reporters were not permitted to accompany the expedition and had to rely instead on brief messages relayed by Colonel James F. Gregory, Sheridan's aide-de-camp. Several large newspapers responded to the demand for news of the presidential party by manufacturing stories from their "own correspondent[s] with the President." The so-called dispatches were often confusing and contradictory. The President's standing with the fourth estate suffered substantially because he had not invited newsmen to accompany him. But Arthur did not contemplate running for election in 1884 and was not particularly concerned with press relations. During the short period he was away from Washington, his main concerns were rest, relaxation, and good fishing.[5]

Throughout the last two decades of the nineteenth century, scientific interest in northwestern Wyoming increased. The U.S. Geological Survey and the U.S. Fish Commission sent many expeditions into the area. Two government scientific parties—Arnold Hague's in 1884[6] and Barton W. Evermann's in 1891[7]—examined the topography, geology, fish, and wildlife in northern Jackson Hole.

The curiosity of private individuals, especially big-game hunters, regarding this remote northwest corner of Wyoming also grew during the period. Jackson Hole had always held a reputation as a hunter's paradise, first for the Indians, later for European noblemen, and by the 1880's for American sportsmen as well. During the fur-trade era, a wealthy Scotsman, Captain William Drummond Stewart of Murthlie Castle, had been lured to Jackson Hole by tales of fabulous hunting. A fictionalized version of his pleasant experiences in the valley was published in 1846.[8] Another European, William A. Baillie-Grohman, followed Stewart's example and hunted the Jackson Hole country in the 1870's[9] and again in 1880.[10] His success, especially in bagging an excellent trophy elk in the Gros Ventre Mountains, encouraged other European hunters—including two Austrian counts, Ernst Hoyos and Ferdinand Trautmannsdorf —to visit the area.

In 1896 and 1897, F. Jay Haynes accompanied two elaborate safaris into Jackson Hole, both financed by American railroad magnate W. Seward Webb. Haynes's photographs attest to the success of Webb and his wealthy hunting partners.[11] The most reliable information regarding the quality of hunting in Jackson Hole, however, came from Beaver Dick Leigh, who had roamed there for decades. Leigh wrote that in "the butifull valley of Jacksons Hole . . . the game . . . is not to be snesed at for elk and deer and Bare is very plenty." He noted that the region offered "the best hunting that i know of eny ware in the rocky mountains."[12] Dozens of other parties followed Beaver Dick's advice, but written records of their hunting expeditions were rarely kept.

CHAPTER TEN

TRAVAILS OF THE FIRST HOMESTEADERS

While wealthy European noblemen and eastern capitalists were sampling the valley's exceptional hunting and fishing, hunters and trappers of more humble birth and possessions were also coming into Jackson Hole. From this latter group, Jackson Hole gained its first true settlers. Men like Beaver Dick Leigh, John Pierce, Tim Hibbard, and Dave Brackenridge had built temporary cabins in the valley, but not until 1884 did erstwhile trapper John Holland and his friend John Carnes establish the first permanent homesteads there. The two hauled crude farm machinery and other supplies on pack horses over the divide from Green River, across Bacon Creek, and down the Gros Ventre to their cabins near Flat Creek. In succeeding years, a number of pioneers, including John Cherry, J. Pierce Cunningham, John Hicks, Stephen N. Leek, Robert E. Miller, Martin Nelson, and

Dick Turpin, took up permanent or semipermanent residence in Jackson Hole. By 1889, there were approximately forty settlers, many of them in their early twenties, living in the valley.

In the fall of 1889, the first authentic wagon train, carrying five Mormon families from Utah, entered Jackson Hole over Teton Pass. The caravan included fifty-year-old Sylvester Wilson, his wife Mary, son Joseph, and daughters Ella and Rebecca; Sylvester's son Ervin Wilson, wife Mary Jane, and son Jim; Sylvester's son-in-law Selar Cheney, wife Mary, and children; Sylvester's brother Elijah N. "Uncle Nick" Wilson, wife Matilda, and daughter Kate; and Elijah's married daughter Louise Smith and her two boys. Drought had driven the Wilson clan north from Utah into Idaho, where conditions were not much better. When they heard of a wetter climate east of the Tetons, the Wilsons decided to settle in Jackson Hole, where their starving livestock could graze on the abundant wild hay of that region.

Although never considered impossible, crossing Teton Pass was certainly a difficult endeavor. It should be recalled that despite their daring and skill, the early-day trappers had never attempted to ascend or descend the pass in wheeled vehicles. The Wilsons were among the first groups to negotiate a successful passage. To ascend the western slope of the Tetons, the men hitched several teams onto each wagon and, one at a time, pulled the heavy-laden vehicles to the summit. Descending the east slope was even more difficult and time consuming. First, the larger rear wheels were interchanged with those in front so that the wagons would not overturn on the steep incline. Then the wheels were chain-locked, and when additional braking power was required, trees were roped to the backs of the wagons and dragged along on the ground. Several members of the party moved ahead of the wagons to clear a path through the timber and rocks. If a fallen tree too large to cut blocked the way, the men piled brush on either side of the trunk and drove right over the top of it.

In Jackson Hole, where colder temperatures and approaching snows left little time to erect cabins, the recently arrived settlers sought shelter in the homes of their new neighbors. Homesteader John Cherry welcomed Ervin Wilson, Ervin's teen-age bride, and their six-week-old baby into his cabin for the winter. Jackson Hole's weather was hard on those early pioneers. When Ervin Wilson's two cows died the first winter, his infant son was relegated to a meager diet of elk soup. The adults relied on wild game, elk and antelope mostly, for their sustenance. By the fall of 1890, however, Ervin's situation was improved. He had purchased a cow and a heifer calf and had constructed a one-room, dirt-floor cabin in South Park, the lush meadow southwest of present-day Jackson. The other members of the Wilson clan were also better off that second winter. In 1891, Effie Jane Wilson, the first white child born in the valley, and Howard Cheney, the first white boy to be born there, arrived. Medical knowledge and supplies were very limited, and not much could be done when two of Sylvester Wilson's younger children contracted diphtheria during the third winter. They were buried in Jackson Hole's first cemetery at South Park.

More homesteaders followed the Wilsons and their predecessors into Jackson Hole. Small settlements grew up at South Park; Wilson, near the base of Teton Pass; Jackson, in the south-central part of the valley; Marysvale, five miles north of Jackson; Zenith, near what is now Jackson Hole Golf Course; Grovont, on Ditch Creek; Kelly, on the Gros Ventre; Moose, where Grand Teton National Park now has its headquarters; Elk, near Spread Creek; Moran, at the outlet of Jackson Lake; and Hoback and Bondurant, along the Hoback River. The pioneer families gained a certain amount of security, practical assistance, and psychological relief by living near each other in such communities.[1]

The settlers of Jackson Hole, like those all across the West, faced many serious problems and responsibilities, most of which could be classified into five categories: food, clothing, shelter, and medicine; transportation and communication; education and religion; law and order; politics and government.

The difficulties of providing food, clothing, shelter, and medicine have been discussed with regard to the Wilson family, and no more need be said here except that all of Jackson Hole's early residents faced similar situations. The nearest supplies of a manufactured sort were available at Rexburg and Idaho Falls, many miles away on the other side of Teton Pass. Trips of such distance and difficulty were made only occasionally during the summer months, and hardly ever once the winter snows had come. Medical attention was especially limited until 1916, when the citizens of Jackson Hole gained their first permanent doctor in the person of Charles W. Huff, a recent graduate of Johns Hopkins Medical School.

For summer transportation, the settlers relied on horses and wagons (often of their own construction); in winter, these were replaced by snowshoes and dogsleds. Like the trappers before them, the settlers were invariably faced with the problem of crossing Jackson Hole's deep streams and rivers, particularly the mighty Snake, which divided the valley almost in half. In the winter, very early spring, and late fall, the waterways were usually low enough for a simple fording. During the warmer months, however, melting snows made the rivers much too rapid and deep for safe crossing. Jackson Holers had to seek other solutions in the form of ferries and bridges.

In 1892, William D. Menor constructed a ferry at Moose along one of the few stretches where the Snake River flows in a single channel. The ferry, a railed platform supported by two pontoons, was guided across the Snake by ropes attached to an overhead cable which was in turn secured to a massive log or "dead man" on shore. The rolling current of the river provided the power to move the ferry, the deck of which was large enough to accommodate a four-horse team and wagon or a large number of livestock. Menor's prices were reasonable: fifty cents for a team and twenty-five cents for a horse and rider. A foot passenger was carried free if a vehicle was crossing at the same time. Each winter, the ferry was hauled ashore and a temporary bridge erected to serve until ferry operations could resume the following spring.[2]

In 1895, a gold-mining concern, prospecting the Whetstone Creek area in northern Jackson Hole, constructed the valley's second ferry. Known as Conrad Ferry for its operator, Ernest Conrad, it consisted of an unrailed, bargelike platform pulled across the Snake River at a point several miles downstream from the Jackson Lake outlet. Operations there ceased in 1897 when Harris-Dunn and Company's placer-mining venture proved unprofitable. A toll bridge was built at near-by Moran to accommodate Conrad's former customers.[3]

During the 1890's, a wagon road gradually developed from general use along the rocky west terrace of the Snake from Menor's to Conrad Ferry and Moran Bridge. Another rough wagon road appeared on the east side of the valley about the same time. Travelers on the latter thoroughfare had to ford the Gros Ventre, Ditch Creek, Spread Creek, and Buffalo River. Steel bridges were not erected in the valley until much later—in 1915 between Jackson and Wilson and in 1927 at Moose. Crude roadways over Teton and Conant passes or through the Hoback and Gros Ventre canyons were the only acceptable ways into or out of the valley until 1898, when the army responded to an Indian scare in the region by building a military road over Togwotee Pass.[4]

Communication was nearly as great a problem as transportation for the citizens of Jackson Hole. Mail came as far as the railroad depot on the Idaho side of Teton Pass and from there was carried on horseback or snowshoes (depending on the season) to Jackson. A number of hardy individuals then distributed letters and packages to the various post offices which had sprung up around the valley. Aside from those infrequent mail deliveries, Jackson Holers were generally out of touch with the outside world. Contact among themselves was also restricted, though the founding, in 1909, of the first newspaper, the *Jackson's Hole Courier*, remedied the intravalley communication problem to a considerable extent.

Like transportation and communication, education was a problem and a responsibility for the people of Jackson Hole. The Mormon emigrants of 1889 had resolved that their children would not be denied the benefits of formal learning. The first classes were held in the South Park homestead cabins of the Wilson clan, and in 1896 a one-room log schoolhouse was erected on Ervin Wilson's property in South Park. Each father built desks and benches for his children. Miss Susie Clark of Idaho Falls was hired by the education-minded settlers to teach a three-month term when the school first opened.

Settlers in other parts of the valley followed South Park's example, and by 1905, schoolhouses were operating at Flat Creek, Wilson, Grovont, Zenith, and Jackson. Sessions became longer—three months in the fall and three in the spring—and attendance grew markedly. In 1914, Jackson built a four-room brick schoolhouse, and because of the increased number of older children attending, a high school gradually evolved.

Education in Jackson Hole was a community project. Everyone shared proportionally in the cost of building, heating, and furnishing the school buildings and paying the teachers. In 1921, the Jackson Parent-Teacher Association was organized to guarantee that this form of close community co-operation would continue.

Jackson Holers were also concerned with organized religion. The settlers of South Park held the first Mormon service on Easter Sunday, 1890, in Sylvester Wilson's homestead cabin. Four years later, they moved to a log church near by for their services. Not many years passed before Jackson added its first Mormon church, as well as Episcopal and Baptist churches, to its growing number of stores, hotels, and saloons. Houses of worship eventually appeared throughout the valley in the various centers of settlement, particularly Mormon Row, the string of Mormon homesteads along the east side of Blacktail Butte.

CHAPTER ELEVEN

OUTLAWS, VIGILANTES, AND THE INDIAN MASSACRE

Like any young community, Jackson Hole had a certain amount of difficulty in maintaining law and order among its citizens. Furthermore, because of its isolated mountain setting, the valley was occasionally troubled by lawbreakers from outside communities who sought refuge there. This is not to say that most of the people living in Jackson Hole were criminals; far from it. In fact, most residents were generally law-abiding. Only a few of them had ever run seriously afoul of the law. Unfortunately, dime novelists and others extrapolated upon the experiences of those few and created for the valley an exaggerated reputation as a haven for criminals. Some writers probably confused Jackson Hole with Hole-in-the-Wall, a blind canyon in north-central Wyoming which outlaws were known to frequent. In any case, Jackson Hole's reputation for lawlessness still attracts many modern-day tourists. For that reason, if for no other, the true story of crime and civil disorder there should be told.

In the valley dwelt a few men who, because of their strange habits and unknown past, were thought to be fugitives from the law. One of them was "Uncle Jack" Davis, a recluse miner on Bailey Creek, Snake River Canyon, who had purportedly fled to Jackson Hole from the Montana gold camps after killing a man in a barroom brawl.[1] Another man in the region bore the unlikely name of "Teton Jackson." Stories about him were confused and contradictory. Some people said he rustled horses; others, cattle. Still others claimed he was a respected rancher, and one person thought he was a bank director.[2] A newspaper article[3] dated October 12, 1886, claimed that in May of that year, Jackson and his henchman, "Blackie Marks," had stolen thirty-nine head of horses in Idaho and driven them east (probably through Jackson Hole), only to be arrested in Bighorn Basin, Wyoming Territory. Jackson reportedly confessed to being the leader of a band of horse thieves, whose hideout "was a strongly built log house in the center of a morass [Flat Creek swamplands?] in Jackson's Hole which could be held against almost anything but artillery." Jackson claimed that homesteaders John Holland and John Carnes had furnished the gang with supplies.

Whatever truth there was in Jackson's confession—and there may have been very little—he became immortalized (though not by name) in American literature because of what he had said. A year after Teton Jackson's capture, Owen Wister visited Jackson Hole and heard about the valley's notorious horse thief.[4] When he later wrote *The Virginian,* that classic western novel which was the first to draw a lasting prototype of the American cowboy ("When you call me that, smile!"), Wister incorporated into it the spirit, if not the deeds, of Teton Jackson and his fellow desperadoes. Chapter 33 began:

Somewhere at the eastern base of the Tetons did those hoofprints disappear into a mountain sanctuary where many crooked paths have led. He that took another man's possessions, or he that took another man's life, could always run here if the law or popular justice were too hot at his heels. Steep ranges and forests walled him in from the world on all four sides, almost without a break; and every entrance lay through intricate solitudes. Snake River came into the place through cañons and mournful pines and marshes, to the north, and went out at the south between formidable chasms. Every tributary to this stream rose among high peaks and ridges, and descended into the valley by well-nigh impenetrable courses: Pacific Creek from Two Ocean Pass, Buffalo Fork from no pass at all, Black Rock from the To-wo-ge-tee Pass—all these, and many more, were the waters of loneliness, among whose thousand hiding-places it was easy to be lost. Down in the bottom was a spread of level land, broad and beautiful, with the blue and silver Tetons rising from its chain of lakes to the west, and other heights presiding over its other sides. And up and down and in and out of this hollow square of mountains where waters plentifully flowed, and game and natural pasture abounded, there skulked a nomadic and distrustful population. This in due time built cabins, took wives, begot children, and came to speak of itself as "The honest settlers of Jackson's Hole." It is a commodious title, and doubtless to-day more accurate than it was once.

In to this place the hoofprints disappeared. Not many cabins were yet built there; but the unknown rider of the horse knew well that he would find shelter and welcome among the felons of his stripe. Law and order might guess his name correctly, but there was no next step, for lack of evidence; and he would wait, whoever he was, until the rage of popular justice, which had been pursuing him and his brother thieves, should subside. Then, feeling his way gradually with prudence, he would let himself be seen again.[5]

A third fabled lawbreaker in the Jackson Hole country was Edwin H. Trafton, alias Ed Harrington, who served two sentences for horse theft and another for robbing his own mother. He was well known in the northern end of the valley and once lived in a cabin near Colter Bay.[6] Trafton's most notable feat was the singlehanded daylight robbery of fifteen Yellowstone Park stagecoaches on July 29, 1914. For his efforts, he received a rapid arrest, lighthearted editorial recognition as far east as New York,[7] and five years in Leavenworth Prison.

Despite the presence among them of men like Davis, Jackson, and Trafton, the more self-respecting citizens of Jackson Hole were always ready (sometimes overeager) to exercise their vigilante power in order to maintain law and order in the valley. The so-called Affair at Cunningham's Ranch demonstrated their readiness. In the fall of 1892, two strangers, Mike Burnett and George Spencer, rode into Jackson Hole with a string of horses and inquired about the possibilities of purchasing hay. Pioneer settler J. Pierce Cunningham sold them some and offered them winter accommodations on his Spread Creek ranch in the north end of the valley. Cunningham himself spent the winter with friends in south Jackson Hole.

During the next few months, rumors spread through the valley that Burnett and Spencer were horse thieves. The following spring, a man claiming to be a United States marshal from Idaho and several men claiming to be his deputies rode into the valley, ostensibly looking for horse thieves. A dozen Jackson Holers informed the posse of Burnett's and Spencer's whereabouts and agreed to lead the supposed lawmen to Cunningham's cabin. The posse reached the cabin at daybreak, surprised Burnett and Spencer, and opened fire on the two men before any explanations could be made. Both Burnett and Spencer were killed after a short gun battle and were buried on a near-by knoll.

Although no one seems to have considered the possibility at the time, Burnett and Spencer may have been innocent victims of mistaken identity or, worse yet, a diabolical plot. It is altogether possible that the two men were honest horsemen victimized by unfounded rumors and a band of Idaho horse thieves masquerading as law-enforcement officers. Such incidents were not unknown in the early West. When questioned by historian Fritiof Fryxell years later, the surviving Jackson Hole members of the posse, of course, insisted on Burnett's and Spencer's guilt, but the full truth of the affair will probably never be known. No trial or inquest was held, and the horses were immediately returned to Idaho with the "marshal." One bit of later conversation hinted that he may not have been a lawman: none of the Jackson Hole posse members could remember ever having seen his official identification papers or his written arrest warrants, both of which he should have been carrying on his person.[8]

The Affair at Cunningham's Ranch may have been Jackson Hole's first great miscarriage of justice. Even if the verdict of bullets could be called just, the methods of the armed jury can hardly be condoned. They can, however, be better understood in the light of another decision handed down six years before. In 1887, John Tonnar was acquitted

Cathedral Group across String Lake

The Maud Noble cabin at Moose, where Yellowstone Park Superintendent Horace Albright heard local conservationists propose the creation of a Jackson Hole recreation area

Horace M. Albright, superintendent of Yellowstone National Park, at Tower Falls about 1925

Horace M. Albright with Crown Prince Gustav Adolf (Gustav IV) of Sweden, at Fishing Peale Island, Yellowstone National Park, 1926. After this fishing sojourn Albright took the crown prince and princess to a dude ranch in Jackson Hole.

Harold P. Fabian (left), an attorney retained by John D. Rockefeller, Jr., and Horace M. Albright (right) at Fabian's summer home between Moose and Jenny Lake about 1955

(Top) The Prather property, north of Spread Creek, before purchase
by the Rockefeller-owned Snake River Land Company
(Below) The Prather property about 1945, after the Rockefeller land-
clearing activities

John D. Rockefeller, Jr.,
about 1935

Plaque on Lunch Tree Hill near Jackson Lake Lodge

View of the western slope of the Tetons from Paintbrush Ridge.
Grand Teton is at the right.

of the charge of having murdered his three gold-mining partners along a stretch of the Snake River in Jackson Hole. The evidence introduced at Tonnar's trial—held in Evanston, the county seat of Uinta County, of which Jackson Hole was then a part—though overwhelmingly against him, was solely circumstantial. The jury was not convinced beyond a reasonable doubt, and Tonnar was freed. A reconstruction of the details of the grisly triple murder, however, makes Tonnar appear guilty despite the jury's verdict.

Tonnar and his three partners, Henry Welter, T. H. Tiggerman, and August Kellenberger, went to Jackson Hole from Montana in the spring of 1886. They established placer operations on a timbered gravel bar—known ever after as Deadman's Bar—below modern-day Snake River Overlook on the Jackson Hole Highway. Nothing was heard from the four men until Tonnar appeared in Pierre's Hole, claiming he had sold out his partnership and was looking for more profitable employment. A rancher hired Tonnar to cut hay, and it was while working in the fields that Tonnar was arrested. Apparently, a boating party had discovered the mutilated bodies of Tonnar's partners partly submerged in the water near their diggings. They had been murdered, one at a time, in their sleep. Welter had an ax cut in the head, Tiggerman's skull was crushed, and two bullets were lodged in Kellenberger's back. Tonnar was the natural suspect. He never confessed to the crime, of course, but the fact that he expressed no sorrow over the fate of his former comrades and the fact that he disappeared from Wyoming immediately after his acquittal made many settlers suspicious. Perhaps the citizens of Jackson Hole learned from the episode at Deadman's Bar that peaceful courtroom methods sometimes seemed to impede justice. The experiences of 1886–87 might explain the settlers' eagerness to deal hastily and extralegally with future lawbreakers, such as the two unfortunate young men at Cunningham's cabin in 1893.[9]

Another example of the Jackson Holers' hasty and often ill-conceived pursuit of justice occurred in 1895. This time the lawbreakers were Indians. By the mid-1890's, most of America's Indians had been assigned to various reservations throughout the West. While they were supposed to spend most of their time on the reservations proper, the Indians were often granted temporary passes which entitled them to visit neighboring reservations and to hunt wild game en route. Bannocks from the Fort Hall Reservation west of Teton Pass and Shoshonis from the Wind River Reservation used their passes to hunt elk in Jackson Hole. The practice irritated the white residents of Jackson Hole for several reasons. First, the whites were afraid of and prejudiced against any armed red men hunting or camping in the vicinity of white homesteads. Second, Indian hunters reduced the number of trophy elk available to local white hunters and to rich eastern patrons on whose guide fees many local whites depended. Third, the state of Wyoming had certain seasonal game laws which every hunter was obliged to obey but which Indian hunters blatantly disobeyed. For years, outraged Jackson Hole residents had complained in vain to their governor and to the U.S. Commissioner of Indian Affairs about Indians hunting illegally. Bureaucratic defenders of the red men pointed out that treaties granting Indians the right to hunt on all unoccupied lands, regardless of season, were superior to state game laws which prohibited hunting out of season.

Failing to get help from Washington, the Jackson Holers took matters into their own hands. Justice of the Peace Frank H. Rhoads issued a warrant for the arrest of a Bannock hunting party, and Constable William Manning led a posse of twenty-six settlers toward Hoback Canyon to make the arrests. Nine men, thirteen women, and five children were easily captured and marched thirty miles to Marysvale, Jackson Hole, where their rifles, saddles, blankets, tipis, and one horse were confiscated in lieu of cash to pay their fines. On the ride to Marysvale, several white men suddenly loaded their rifles as if to indicate that the captive Indians would be shot in the back. Sensing danger, several braves dashed for cover. The posse believed that the Indians were trying to escape and opened fire. It is not certain whether the Indians were mistaken in believing that they would be shot in the back or whether the whites had deliberately planned their actions so that the Indians would try to escape. In any case, one old Indian was killed, another badly wounded, and the others recaptured.

Not long after the shooting, settlers in Jackson Hole began to fear the consequences of their actions. Scattered throughout the valley in various hunting parties were two or three hundred braves who, if they became vengeful, could wreak destruction on the valley, killing settlers and burning homesteads. The homesteaders gathered inside well-armed stockades at the ranches of Ervin Wilson, Robert Miller, and Pierce Cunningham and telegraphed Washington demanding military protection from imminent disaster. The nation's press picked up the story and exaggerated it completely out of proportion to the truth. Page 1 of the *New York Times* headlined the story: "SETTLERS MASSACRED Indians Kill Every One at Jackson's Hole."[10]

As things turned out, the people of Jackson Hole were not massacred, nor were they ever in any real danger. The Indians were in no mood to fight, and they harbored no illusions about being able to defeat the five companies of

139

the Eighth Cavalry heading for the valley. When the full story became known, most eastern newspapers switched their sympathy to the side of the Indians. Federal officials publicly condemned the citizens of Jackson Hole, for arresting the Indians and intentionally killing one of them. But the governor of Wyoming supported the settlers' action and demanded further legal action against the Bannocks. With the blessing of the commissioner of Indian Affairs, Chief Race Horse from Fort Hall Reservation volunteered for a case. In the first hearing before the U.S. Circuit Court, Judge John A. Riner ruled that the settlers were in the wrong and that the laws of Wyoming were inferior to the prior treaty rights of the Bannocks.[11] On May 25, 1896, however, the U.S. Supreme Court reversed the judgment of the lower court and upheld "the complete power" of a state "to regulate the killing of game within its borders."[12]

Technically, the Supreme Court's ruling justified the acts of Constable Manning and his Jackson Hole posse. In reality, however, there could be no moral or legal justification for the methods which the settlers had employed. When arrested initially, the Indians (few of whom could understand English and all of whom thought hunting in Jackson Hole was their legal right) were not told why they were being held, nor were they offered legal counsel. Moreover, shooting unarmed Indians (even though they appeared to be escaping) was as utterly inexcusable as it would be today if a white policeman shot and killed an Indian youngster for stealing a hubcap. Although the settlers' end—maintenance of the state game laws—was seemingly meritorious, the means to achieve that end were based on a self-centered, immature, and rather shortsighted approach to legal problems. By insisting on a brutal defense of law in the short run, the settlers forsook the traditional legal techniques which are the bulwark of law and justice in the long run.[13]

Only with the passing of time did the citizens of Jackson Hole develop a more sophisticated understanding of the law. There continued to be a certain lack of respect for external legal authority and dependence on vigilante-type justice. In 1901, a posse of Jackson Hole ranchers discovered a sheepherder descending a pass from Idaho, threatened his life, slaughtered some of his stock, and drove his flock out of the valley. The ranchers' justification for their actions was simply that sheep, because they eat grass almost to the roots, would destroy the grazing ranges of elk and cattle, the two animals on which most Jackson Hole natives depended for food and income. Previous successes (1886, 1898) in repelling sheepmen had bolstered the confidence and self-righteousness of the ranchers and had perhaps lessened their belief in slower, more rational legal techniques.[14]

One final vigilante action occurred in 1906 when thirty-five Jackson men chased some elk poachers out of the valley. The gang, headed by William Binkley, Charles Purdy, and Charles Isabel, had slaughtered hundreds of elk in northern Jackson Hole and portions of Yellowstone Park. They left the carcasses to rot and removed the elks' tusks (canine teeth), which could be sold as charms and emblems to members of the Benevolent and Protective Order of Elks (B.P.O.E.), a fraternal organization. Because state game wardens had consistently failed to prosecute the tuskers, the citizens of Jackson Hole felt called upon to halt the practice before the valley's herd was decimated. In contrast to the settlers' previous vigilante conduct, in this case they acted sensibly and moderately. Saner voices prevailed when someone suggested capturing the hunters and executing them without a trial. The settlers' moderation paid off in the long run. After being driven out of Jackson Hole, Purdy and Binkley were captured in Los Angeles, tried, and sentenced. Soon, tusking in Jackson Hole disappeared completely, thanks to the elimination of the Binkley-Purdy-Isabel gang and the B.P.O.E.'s decision to discard tusks as official emblems. Today, remains of tuskers' and other elk poachers' wilderness cabins can be seen along Arizona, Berry, and Glade creeks and near Huckleberry Mountain at the extreme northern end of Jackson Hole.[15]

CHAPTER TWELVE

PETTICOAT RULERS: EQUALITY
ON THE FRONTIER

As the people of Jackson Hole gradually achieved a more mature understanding of law and order, as evidenced in the tusker affair, they began to acknowledge the need for formalized local government. During the early 1900's, each small community in the valley held elections for its own public officials. The town of Jackson, settled in the 1890's, was incorporated in 1914, with Harry Wagner as its first mayor. In 1920, the citizens of that town demonstrated their political maturity and their refreshing sense of equality by electing an all-female slate, the first in American history. Mrs. Grace Miller garnered twice as many votes as Fred Lovejoy in the mayoral race. Mrs. Genevieve Van Vleck, Mrs. Faustina Haight, Mrs. Mae Deloney, and Mrs. Rose Crabtree were the four victorious candidates for town council. Mrs. Crabtree had the additional pleasure of defeating

143

her husband, Henry, who also was a candidate. During their term of office, the town's "petticoat rulers" apparently did an acceptable job—converting country lanes into city streets, acquiring a cemetery site, and investigating plans for a new water and irrigation system. The women were returned for a second term in the 1921 election.[1]

Jackson's novel experiment in municipal government served as a topic for many lighthearted literary efforts across the nation. One newspaper printed a poem entitled "New Rule of Queens," which said in part:

> Where once the powder
> Smoke from "forty-fives"
> Rose in the air, to
> Check our reckless lives;
>
> Now powder puffs flash
> Forth in dainty hand,
> To rule the bad
> Men of our land.
>
> And cowboy brave
> And fighting man
> All wilt before
> The perfumed fan.[2]

The Jackson elections were meaningful not merely because they signaled the passing of the Old West, nor for the precedent which they established for voters in the rest of the United States, but because of the deeper sociological significance that lay behind the electorate's decision. It was not coincidence that the first town in America to have an all-female government was a western town. Nor was it coincidence that a western state, Wyoming, was the first state in the union to grant women suffrage. More than any other factor, the pioneer experience prepared westerners to accept the idea of female equality. Women had earned equal rights with men by performing so well amidst the harsh realities of frontier life. Women had borne and reared children under the most trying circumstances. They had fought alongside their husbands in Indian raids. They had helped to hitch wagons, saddle horses, plow fields, and build cabins. When their husbands were away or dead, they performed all the necessary tasks required for existence. Of course, women on the frontier had never demonstrated equal *physical* strength, but in terms of *mental* strength—determination and will to survive—women had clearly shown men that they were equals. Men and women, husbands and wives, had acted as partners in the settlement of the West. Therefore, it was natural for them to become partners in the political future and economic progress of the West. Jackson Hole was one of the areas in which that partnership first became manifest.

With the election of an all-female government, Jackson Hole turned its back on an old world to face a new one, a world in which exploration and settlement were no longer the dominant themes. The difficulties of providing food, clothing, shelter, and medicine and the accompanying problems of transportation and communication had been largely solved. Institutions of education, religion, law, and government had been firmly established. Two new themes, commercialization and conservation, were now coming into focus, each attempting to exclude the other. Neither was entirely new. The fur trappers of bygone days had participated in a type of commercialization, and the vigilante committees of more recent times had acted (especially in regard to the elk tuskers) like many modern advocates of conservation. But in the most recent chapter of Jackson Hole's history, these twin themes, commercialization and conservation, have taken on a broader scope and a larger significance and have wrought greater conflict than the trappers or vigilantes would have ever dreamed possible.

Part III **COMMERCIALIZATION AND CONSERVATION**

CHAPTER THIRTEEN

SETTLERS' LIVELIHOODS

The chief occupation of Jackson Hole's early settlers was the raising of beef cattle and hay to feed them during the winter. The first herd was brought into Jackson Hole in the mid-1880's. With frequent rains providing a dependable source of water and with enough fertile soil to grow an adequate grass supply, many sections of Jackson Hole were admirably suited for cattle ranching. The time-honored western scene—roundup, branding iron, dusty cowboy and pony—became an intimate part of the valley's history, and experienced cowhands could often be seen driving market-bound steers over the Tetons to railroad depots in Idaho.[1]

To supplement their income, a few ranchers and their sons doubled as guides and outfitters for parties of eastern and European hunters. Other Jackson Holers made guiding a full-time occupation. Ben Sheffield built a wagon road around the northern and eastern extremities of Jackson Lake to ease the difficulty of getting clients and supplies into Jackson Hole. He maintained an extensive guide service at Moran. His expeditions shot countless trophy animals throughout the northern valley and in the mountains immediately south of Yellowstone Park. Before Sheffield's time, others had operated less formal guide facilities in the valley. Stephen Leek once ran a hunting camp at the north end of Jackson Lake.[2] And even before Leek, two easterners named Ray Hamilton and John Sargent had built on its shore an elaborate guest cabin replete with ten finely furnished rooms, including a classical library. Known as Merymere, the cabin still stands on the AMK Ranch.[3]

Those wealthy sportsmen who packed through Jackson Hole and stayed at Merymere and Leek's camp and in Sheffield's cabins could not readily forget the inspiring beauty of the valley. Many returned with their families to build summer ranches. One celebrated returnee was Philadelphia novelist Owen Wister, who had packed into the region in 1887, 1891, and 1893. He came back in 1911 with his wife and children and returned again the following year to build a two-story cabin on the present-day R Lazy S Ranch between Moose and Wilson.[4]

For families who did not own ranches, there developed a new kind of accommodation: the dude ranch. Jackson Hole's first, the JY, was started on Phelps Lake in 1908 by Louis H. Joy. Four years later, Struthers Burt, a writer from Philadelphia who had been associated with Joy's endeavor, joined another Philadelphian, Dr. Horace Carncross, to found Jackson Hole's second dude ranch, the Bar BC, on the west bank of the Snake north of Moose. Other dude outfits—the White Grass, Double Diamond, Tri-angle X, and Circle H—soon followed.[5]

For well-heeled city folks who could afford it, a dude ranch vacation was a marvelous adventure likely to evoke fond memories for years to come. There was that first ex-posure to horses, certainly less pleasant than the greenhorn had anticipated. But once he conquered his rather thinly concealed fear of being thrown and adjusted to the initially repulsive sounds and smells of four-footed companions, he developed a close and almost romantic relationship with his mount. The thrills of galloping across the sagebrush, splashing through streams, and plodding up cool wood-land trails were not likely to be forgotten. Nor would the dude forget the night he camped on the Tetons at the seeming edge of heaven or the breakfast of pancakes and bacon with which he stuffed himself the morning after. He would remember his companions and the gala party held at the ranch near the end of the summer. And, of course, there was the inevitable skunk who hid himself under one of the cabins and defied all efforts at removal.

Visitors themselves furnished the most effective mode of advertisement for Jackson Hole. Invariably they told their friends back home about the valley's clean air, re-markable scenery, and splendid fishing and wildlife. Trumped-up tales of bygone trappers and horse thieves added to the area's attractions. Applications for summer accommodations grew markedly, and many dude wranglers found their ventures far more profitable than they would ever have expected.[6]

Not all of the valley's residents were inclined toward farming, guiding, or ranching. Naturally, some were in-terested in the financial and industrial potential of their new home. Enterprising individuals erected grocery and hardware stores, hotels, and saloons at Wilson, Kelly, Moran, and Jackson. One opportunist, Robert E. Miller, discovered the need for credit operations in the valley. His first loan—several tons of hay distributed at a rather high rate of interest to the Wilson family during their first Jackson Hole winter—established his reputation as a source of credit. Soon he was acting on an informal basis as financier for the entire region. In 1914, Miller and several prosperous neighbors founded the Jackson State Bank, with Miller as president and Mayor Harry Wagner as cashier. The bank corporation issued stock at $100 a share; capital was listed at $10,000, with no reserves. By September, 1914, assets had risen to $26,000 and the bank was capable of assuming considerable responsibility in the promotion of regional development. Besides acting as a source of credit for ranchers and merchants who wished to establish or expand their enterprises, the bank provided the region with its first safe place for savings deposits and its only dependable specie exchange market. All three banking functions —credit, deposit, and specie exchange—were prerequisites for the economic growth of Jackson Hole.[7]

Some of the valley's pioneers retained their gold-seeking predecessors' interest in mineral resources and industrial stone. A few residents panned for gold dust, but nobody ever discovered the mother lodes from which the stream deposits had undoubtedly come. While searching in vain for primary gold ore, the settler-prospectors encountered coal and phosphate outcrops along Lava Creek, Cache Creek, and the Buffalo and Gros Ventre rivers. The Jackson Hole Coal Company was formed to mine the Upper Gros Ventre deposit but was unable to find enough quality coal to make transportation to industrial centers outside of the valley profitable. Nor were the miners able to sell much of their product to local residents. With forests so close by, Jackson Hole did not offer a good market for coal as a home-heating fuel. In addition to mining small amounts of coal and phosphate, a few Jackson Holers quarried limestone for sale to Jackson proprietors and to Holiday Menor, who operated a lime kiln across the river from his brother's ferry at Moose.[8]

Fortunately, none of the mining and quarrying operations in Jackson Hole were extensive enough to damage or destroy the beauty of the countryside. The valley was spared the dreadful afflictions—open-pit scars, surface subsidence, stream pollution, and collapsing mine buildings—so common to many formerly beautiful mountain areas in the Rockies and the Appalachians.

CHAPTER FOURTEEN

CONSERVATIONISTS' RUMBLINGS AND THE STARVATION OF THE ELK HERD

Though the valley escaped the devastation of mining operations, other forms of commercialization did endanger its scenic splendor. Attempts to dam the waters of Jackson Hole's streams and natural lakes comprised one particularly insidious practice. During the early 1900's, the lack of a cheap and dependable water supply was preventing the development of much potentially productive farmland in Idaho's semiarid Snake River Basin. In 1906, the Federal Reclamation Service (at that time under the control of the U.S. Geological Survey) constructed a rock-filled, log-crib dam at the outlet of Jackson Lake in order to regulate the seasonal flow of water into the Snake River. Water was stored in the much enlarged Jackson Lake reservoir during the wetter months and released whenever the volume of the Snake had become insufficient to supply irrigation ditches on Idaho's Minidoka Project. When the crude structure at the mouth of Jackson Lake washed away in 1910, the U.S. Bureau of Reclamation (successor to the Reclamation Service) erected in its place a much sturdier, reinforced-concrete dam which, with the exception of minor alterations, is still standing today.[1]

Although the dam at the outlet of Jackson Lake provided undeniable benefits, particularly in the production of potatoes and sugar beets, it was an unfortunate creation for several reasons. First, it added a touch of unnaturalness to one of the most beautiful lakes in the world. Second, the resulting reservoir backed up water over a considerable portion of historically and ethnologically significant land. The reservoir covered the ancient Indian and trapper trail leading to Conant Pass and washed away artifacts and other scientifically valuable evidence of Indian campgrounds along the original northern shore of Jackson Lake. Third, the raised waters of the reservoir killed thousands of trees and left their gaunt skeletons to outline the shore. When the dam gates were opened during Idaho's dry season, decaying shoreline vegetation became more conspicuous and a foul-smelling mud appeared on the beach and the formerly submerged tree trunks. Had it not been for the later efforts of the National Park Service in having the shore cleared of dead timber and obtaining assurances that the reservoir would thereafter be held at as constant a level as possible, Jackson Lake would have remained a disgusting eyesore to this day. In the case of Jackson Lake dam, commercialization nearly vanquished the forces of conservation.

The battle between the destroyers and the preservers of nature involved Jackson Hole's other lakes and streams. The Cheyenne-based Teton Irrigation Company, acting under the provisions of the federal Carey Land Act of 1894, obtained damming privileges on Spread Creek and the Buffalo and Gros Ventre rivers in 1909 and 1912. The Carey Act provided for donation of up to one million acres of federally owned arid lands to each state having such lands, on condition that the state cause the lands to be reclaimed and settled in small tracts by legitimate home-steaders. Wyoming accepted the land donation and per-mitted the Teton Irrigation Company to furnish water to settlers in the semiarid northeastern portion of Jackson Hole and to collect annual rental fees from them. In theory, water dammed by the company was to be used solely for irrigating Wyoming lands, but through certain unethical and perhaps illegal maneuvers, the firm man-aged to save most of its water for sale (at much higher prices) to Idaho interests. Settlers attracted to northeast-ern Jackson Hole by the prospect of irrigated farmland found the soil there unfit for agricultural use. After futile efforts to make the land productive, most of them aban-doned their homesteads and left the Teton Irrigation Company with a surplus of stored water. Many conserva-tion-minded Jackson Holers felt the firm had tricked Wyoming's state engineers into alloting worthless land for irrigation and settlement. The natives accused company officials of knowing beforehand that the land could not be permanently settled and planning in the long run to sell all of the irrigation water in Idaho. Not until the 1930's did the state suspend the firm's operations in the valley.[2]

The Teton Irrigation Company was not the only private concern to use reclamation laws in such a way as to threaten the natural beauty of Jackson Hole. The Osgood Land and Livestock Company of Idaho and the Utah-Idaho

Sugar Company held similar water-storage and irrigation privileges on Emma Matilda and Two Ocean lakes. The dams the two firms built were not removed until the 1950's when Emma Matilda and Two Ocean were included in the national park system. A third group contemplated a project which would have destroyed for all time the virgin splendor of Jenny and Leigh lakes. Fortunately, however, in the early 1920's, in response to persistent pressure from the National Park Service and Jackson Hole dude ranchers, the Wyoming state engineers halted the project.[3]

Dude rancher Struthers Burt, one of the leading local proponents of conservation, was particularly vociferous in his opposition to the damming of Jackson Hole's lakes and streams. He wrote that the promoters of irrigation and land development schemes

are sleepless and one never knows where they are going to attack next. There is not a valuable future asset in the West to-day, not a lake or a watershed or a forest, the conservation of which is necessary to the health and wealth and security of future generations which is not in danger from forces who do not care a snap of their fingers for future generations so long as they can gut and fell and dam and fill their own pockets.[4]

Today, some portions of Jackson Hole are lined with unsightly irrigation ditches, wooden headgates, and diversion dams. The National Park Service has eliminated most of the remnants of irrigation projects on its lands west of the Snake, but on property east of the Snake it permits the irrigation of hay fields. Also in recent years, because of certain legal commitments between itself and holders of grazing privileges and tenancy agreements, the

Park Service has had to build small irrigation dams on Spread Creek and the Gros Ventre River.

The problem of preserving the natural beauty of Jackson Hole's lakes and waterways has no simple solution. The difficulty is not deciding between a clear-cut "good" (conservation) and an obvious "evil" (commercialization). In the case of irrigation projects, commercialization is not so bad. Its more obvious benefits are reflected in the improved productivity of dry areas and the greater economic well-being of the people who live there. Reclamation helps the entire nation by making useful soil out of wasteland and productive citizens out of those who might otherwise be subsistence farmers and welfare recipients. But reclamation at the expense of one of the most naturally beautiful valleys in the world ought to be carefully controlled and held to an absolute minimum. The preservation of Jackson Hole's unique lakes and streams should be of primary concern, and the agricultural productivity of certain parts of Jackson Hole and Idaho—that productivity being valuable but not unique—should be of secondary importance.

The threat of dams and irrigation projects prompted many Jackson Hole residents (especially dude ranchers, guides, and outfitters) whose livelihoods depended on the continued wildness and beauty of the valley to advocate preservation of the valley as a national or state-owned recreation area. But they were by no means the first people to favor government protection for their magnificent country. As early as 1897, chronic fire danger in the woodlands flanking Jackson Hole had resulted in the creation of Teton Forest Reserve under U.S. Interior Department administration. The reserve encompassed the sagebrush flats of northern Jackson Hole, as well as certain forest lands bordering on the north, northeast, and northwest.

Before the reserve was established, forest fires had ravaged the area, destroying much valuable timber and subjecting the watershed to soil erosion. One particularly severe fire in 1879 had so thoroughly swept the valley that by 1897 only very young trees could be found there. Army surveillance and fire-control units, operating under orders from a forest reserve administrator (as similar units operated in Yellowstone under command of the park superintendent), seemed to offer the best means of safeguarding Jackson Hole's youthful timber. Federal jurisdiction in the reserve extended only to trees and waterways; wild game remained under state control, a condition which immediately led to difficulties.[5]

In his reports to the Secretary of the Interior for 1897, Colonel S. B. M. Young, acting superintendent of Yellowstone Park, complained that large segments of the Yellowstone elk herd were migrating south each winter into the northern end of Jackson Hole, where poachers threatened to decimate the herd. Since migration patterns are habitual and not easily altered, Young suggested that the animal protection provided by troops in Yellowstone Park be extended to the migration paths and the winter grazing lands south of the park. State protection for elk migrating across the park's boundaries had proved ineffective, and Young believed that only extension of those boundaries and establishment of federally enforced no-hunting regulations in northern Jackson Hole's winter feeding grounds could guarantee the survival of the herd. It was senseless, Young stated, to protect the elk vigorously while they were inside Yellowstone Park and then passively accept their wholesale destruction once they left it.[6]

After touring the Jackson Hole country in 1898, Charles D. Walcott, director of the U.S. Geological Survey, concurred in Superintendent Young's recommendations. But Walcott also suggested the possibility of creating a separate Teton National Park to include all of Jackson Hole north of Blacktail Butte. Young's and Walcott's suggestions were communicated to Congress, but no legislation was forthcoming.[7]

From 1898 to 1902, the elk slaughter continued unabated. Law-abiding guides and outfitters, who considered the slaughter a threat to their livelihood, organized a protective association to assist state game wardens in the enforcement of Wyoming's hunting laws. John D. Sargent, owner of Merymere Lodge on Jackson Lake, wrote the commissioner of the General Land Office in Washington about blatant game-law violations committed by settlers who, he claimed, had never made official homestead entries. He named four men whom he considered notorious poachers. Subsequent investigations by an army officer and a forest inspector revealed that at least fourteen squatters, who had cabins in the northern end of Jackson Hole within the boundaries of Teton Forest Reserve, were violating state game regulations by hunting without licenses, by exceeding the open season limit of two elk, and by killing during the closed season. It was discovered that many of the elk were being slaughtered, not for local meat consumption, but for shipments of hides, scalps, and tusks to commercial interests outside the valley.[8]

In their annual reports from 1898 to 1902, the secretary of the Interior and the commissioner of the General Land Office requested extension of Yellowstone's borders so that the park's elk herd could migrate and graze year round in a federally protected area. In 1902, the former drafted a bill incorporating Superintendent Young's original recommendations, but it was never formally acted upon by Congress.[9]

Meanwhile, federal protection of timber was broadened to include all of Jackson Hole's wooded sections. Teton Forest Reserve was enlarged in 1902, and the following year it became, for a time, part of the enormous Yellowstone Forest Reserve. Then, on July 1, 1908, an executive order established the 1,991,200-acre Teton National Forest, encompassing the original Teton Forest Reserve as well as territory to the south. The forest, with headquarters at Robert Miller's ranch on Flat Creek, was placed under the supervision of the Department of Agriculture's Forest Service.[10] As federal concern for Jackson Hole's timber resources grew, Washington's interest in park extension temporarily declined. Protection of wildlife migrating south out of Yellowstone devolved entirely on state authorities. In 1905, the conservation-minded Wyoming Legislature took the initiative by setting aside a 570,000-acre strip north of Moran—the Teton Game Preserve—in which all hunting was prohibited. The next year, the Jackson Hole vigilantes helped state wardens run a gang of elk tuskers out of the preserve.[11]

During the unusually severe winter of 1908–1909, the Jackson Hole elk problem entered a more complicated phase as a blanket of unusually deep snow buried the valley's native forage and threatened thousands of elk with starvation. Since the 1880's a large portion of the elk herd summering in Yellowstone Park had wintered in Jackson Hole. For centuries before that, the animals had merely migrated through Jackson Hole on their way to the warmer grasslands of the Green River Basin. But with the appearance of ranches and barbed-wire fences along Green River in the early 1880's, the elk began to avoid the warmer basin in favor of less densely settled Jackson Hole. Weather on the new winter range tended to be more severe than that on

Green River, and the elk suffered tremendously as a result. By causing the artificial shortening of migration routes, civilization seemed to be endangering the animals' very existence.

In that terrible winter of 1908–1909, elk carcasses littered the countryside and living skeletons of once noble specimens wandered aimlessly through the snow. A few Jackson Holers proffered hay to the starving elk, but most of their grain store had to be reserved for domestic stock. Fences were constructed around haystacks to keep the desperate animals away. Rancher Stephen Leek, an ingenious man with a camera, sought to publicize their tragic plight. His remarkable pictures appeared in several magazines and newspapers and were otherwise circulated around the nation. Many people learned for the first time of Jackson Hole and its elk herd and were alarmed at what appeared to be the herd's impending extinction.

In response to the widespread public concern engendered by Leek's efforts, the Wyoming Legislature appropriated $5,000 worth of grain. Congress followed suit in 1911 with a $20,000 appropriation toward hay purchases. During the succeeding two years, Congress bought property along Flat Creek above Jackson totaling 1,760 acres and added 1,040 acres of unentered public land to form the National Elk Refuge. Additional government purchases and donations by the Izaak Walton League in 1927 and John D. Rockefeller, Jr., in 1949 have enlarged the refuge to its present size of more than 23,000 acres. Hunting is closely regulated, and each winter tons of hay are distributed to elk grazing there. As a result of carefully controlled hunting seasons and winter feeding programs, Jackson Hole's 15,000 elk—one of the larger wild animal herds in the world—need never fear extinction.[12]

CHAPTER FIFTEEN

THE PARK SERVICE ARRIVES

The campaign to save the elk reawakened Washington's interest in park status for Jackson Hole. As a rather fortunate coincidence, members of Congress and the Interior Department were at that very time planning a separate national park bureau which could channel such interest into concrete action. Enabling legislation for the National Park Service, as it was called, was passed in 1916; shortly thereafter, Stephen T. Mather, who had been assistant to the secretary of Interior, was appointed director. Mather chose Horace M. Albright, a young lawyer who had been working in the department since 1913, to be his assistant. Together, these two men shaped the Park Service into an efficient, expanding organization and fought the enemies of conservation on every front. More than anyone else, they

163

were responsible for the wonderful system of national parks enjoyed by millions today.[1]

Before passage of the National Park Service bill, Mather and Albright made a fact-finding tour of Yellowstone Park. They discovered that its boundaries failed to conform to topographical features or to animal migration patterns, thus making effective administration of the park extremely difficult. In 1916, when the creation of the Park Service and his own appointment seemed certain, Albright returned to Yellowstone and, as a part of his continuing examination of the park and its environs, traveled south to Ben Sheffield's place at Moran. Like the fur trappers before him, Albright found the Tetons positively enchanting, but like the dudes of his own time, he considered the reclamation project on Jackson Lake revolting.

Albright returned to Washington to help Mather campaign for revision of Yellowstone's boundaries along more logical lines and for inclusion of the Tetons and northern Jackson Hole before commercial projects further defiled the region. They explained to Wyoming's congressional delegation that in 1872 the architects of Yellowstone Park had lacked comprehensive information about the area and were mainly interested in preserving the sections of geologic and thermal phenomena which they knew best. Consequently, the Yellowstone Park Act established a rather arbitrary rectilinear boundary just large enough to assure protection for Yellowstone Canyon, Upper and Lower Yellowstone Falls, and the known geyser basins. Had they possessed more complete information and greater foresight, the creators of the first national park would very likely have included the Thorofare Plateau, on the southeast corner, and the Tetons, Jackson Lake, and much of Jackson Hole.[2]

Wyoming Representative Frank W. Mondell was won

over to the National Park Service's viewpoint and on April 24, 1918, introduced a bill[3] providing for inclusion of the Thorofare country, the Tetons north of Buck Mountain, Jackson Lake, and everything on the east side of the Snake north of the Buffalo. In support of the bill, President Woodrow Wilson withdrew from entry the federal land within that area. Horace Albright revisited Jackson Hole in the summer of 1918 to promote Mondell's proposal among the local inhabitants. In Jackson he made friends with Dick Winger and several old-timers who said they favored the proposal. Mondell's bill was modified in December, 1918, at Interior Department suggestion, to include part of the Falls River Basin just outside the southwest corner of the 1872 rectangle. The new bill[4] received the approval of Colonel Henry S. Graves, chief of the Forest Service, which currently administered the property proposed for transfer, and appeared destined for enactment. The House passed it, but then Idaho sheepmen, learning that the bill would take away their Falls River range and fearing that it would include grazing land on the west slope of the Tetons as well, persuaded Idaho's John Frost Nugent to block the measure on the floor of the Senate. In the jam of proposed legislation created by a filibuster at the close of the Sixty-fifth Congress, a bill could not be advanced for a vote unless all of the senators concurred. Senator Nugent objected to advancement, thus killing a promising conservation measure.[5]

At the first session of the next Congress, Mondell introduced a similar proposal,[6] but deleted the Falls River provision. Albright, who in June, 1919, had been made superintendent of Yellowstone, traveled south to Jackson Hole once again to secure support for park extension. His reception was in marked contrast to that of the previous

165

summer. Since then, the people of Jackson Hole had developed second thoughts about park extension. Despite the provisions of Mondell's bill protecting existing range rights, local cattlemen doubted these would be effective. Grazing had never been permitted in the original Yellowstone rectangle, and it was conceivable that in attempting to uphold the sanctity of an enlarged unit, the National Park Service would not permit grazing in the annexed lands. Moreover, the legislation did not guarantee cattlemen the right to graze their growing herds in areas where they had not been grazed before. The Jackson Hole cattle industry was booming, and ranchers in the southern end of the valley expected land north of the Buffalo (the area encompassed by Mondell's bill) to be their future grazing site. The Park Service felt that the Buffalo watershed should be preserved for summering elk herds. The Jackson Hole Livestock Association hired Dick Winger to write propaganda against the park extension plan and invited cattlemen in other parts of the state to join in a general denunciation of the proposal.[7]

The opposition which confronted Albright came from other sources as well. Forest Service employees feared the loss of jobs which transfer of federal lands to Park Service jurisdiction might entail. Dude ranchers felt park extension would bring paved roads, automobiles, hotels, and hordes of tourists, all of which would detract from the valley's wilderness atmosphere and destroy their business, which thrived in such an environment. Others were concerned because, they felt, so much taxable property would be taken off the county tax rolls that new schools and similar community projects could not be financed. Actually, the land in question was already federal property and not currently taxable by the county. But were the land to be reopened for homestead entry, it could eventually be occupied and become taxable. Certain influential settlers remembered the occasionally arrogant and discourteous behavior of soldiers garrisoned in Yellowstone Park until 1918 and feared its reappearance in Jackson Hole if supervision of the park system ever reverted to the military. In a memorial to Congress, the Wyoming Legislature echoed the sentiments of Jackson Hole residents in opposing park extension. Jealous of their own prerogatives, state lawmakers viewed the park controversy as a battle of states' rights against federal encroachment. In the face of opposition from so many constituents, Representative Mondell felt it expedient to drop his proposal.[8]

It was not long before the unanimity of local opinion against federal conservation efforts was shattered. A devastating drought in the late summer and fall of 1919 drove winter hay prices sky high and placed local cattlemen in financial difficulty. For the ranchers most deeply in debt, the prospect of selling out to the federal government was more appealing than bankruptcy. In any event, the future of stock raising in the valley no longer appeared as bright as it had earlier in the year. For those who had been planning to switch to dude ranching someday, the time seemed ripe.[9]

Horace Albright managed to convince dude wrangler Struthers Burt that park extension would not bring unlimited numbers of roads and motorists. The inevitable improvement of transportation facilities would be adapted to Jackson Hole's unique frontier atmosphere. In 1920, the towns of Casper and Lander, anxious for a share of the Yellowstone tourist traffic, successfully agitated for improvement of the southern access route, which crossed Togwotee Pass and joined the old road around Jackson Lake. The Park Service rebuilt the Jackson Hole section and constructed a bridge across the Buffalo at Turpin Meadows. Its Washington office planned to shorten the route by cutting a roadway up Pacific Creek and over Two Ocean Pass,[10] but at the request of guides and dude ranchers who wanted to keep the Two Ocean region wild, Superintendent Albright nipped that plan in the bud. The area he saved is now part of the marvelous Teton Wilderness Area, where motorized vehicles, even snowmobiles, are prohibited.[11]

In other respects, Albright demonstrated to the dude industry that the Park Service, unlike the Forest Service and the state, could preserve Jackson Hole from commercial intrusion. The drought of 1919 had created a substantial market for private irrigation schemes and had supplied the production-minded Wyoming state engineer's office with political and economic reasons for encouraging construction of dams, ditches, and headgates in Jackson Hole. Albright lobbied vigorously against the irrigation program and was influential in getting the state to prohibit enlargement of the dams on Emma Matilda and Two Ocean lakes.

Even more crucial to the future of Jackson Hole was the Park Service's fight against a scheme to dam Jenny and Leigh lakes. Applications made to the federal government regarding the project were rejected at the Park Service's suggestion. For additional insurance, Albright argued before Wyoming authorities that water-storage permits should not be issued.[12] In a neat retreat from previous policy,[13] State Engineer Frank Emerson admitted the overwhelming scenic value of the two lakes and refused to allow the damming scheme to go through.[14]

Meanwhile, in Washington, Director Mather waged a battle against proposed reclamation projects in the existing national parks. Irrigation interests were on the verge of damming Yellowstone and neighboring lakes within the park when Congress, at Mather's instigation, exempted the park system from the provisions of the 1920 Water Power Act, which opened all federal lands to reclamation projects.[15]

Drought, irrigation schemes, and the growing number of unsightly tourist facilities near Jenny Lake led local men to reconsider the future of their region. After mulling over the problem at Joe Jones's Jackson store, several residents concluded that the most logical and effective way to combat commercialization was to transform Jackson Hole into a government-supervised or government-owned recreation area. Struthers Burt invited Superintendent Albright to visit Jackson Hole and help its conservation-minded citizens draw up plans to protect the valley. Meeting in Miss Maud Noble's cabin at Moose on July 26, 1923, Albright discussed the possibilities of a national recreation area with Burt, Jones, Horace Carncross, Jack Eynon, and Dick Winger. The local men agreed that all of the valley—from rim to rim—should be included in the proposed recreation area. However, they also agreed that Jackson Hole should not be accorded status as a national park. It should continue to have hunting, grazing, and dude ranching on limited scales. In this way it could become a "museum on the hoof," a living example of life in the Old West. Albright did not abandon his dream of a great Yellowstone Park extending into Jackson Hole, but he was content to go along with the Noble cabin proposal as a possible step toward the ultimate realization of that dream.[16]

The major obstacle to the success of the plan was lack of money. Thousands of dollars' worth of land and improvements had to be purchased before a Jackson Hole national recreation area could be established. Congress was in no mood to appropriate funds, and local landowners could hardly be expected to donate their property and dismantle their buildings, even if they were sympathetic to the general idea. Dick Winger and Jack Eynon spent two months in the East soliciting private contributions from wealthy individuals who had hunted and vacationed in Jackson Hole. Although their audiences were receptive to the Noble cabin idea, Winger and Eynon secured little financial help.[17]

In 1924, the President's Committee on Outdoor Recreation appointed a co-ordinating commission to consider a number of boundary adjustments between national forests and national parks. During the summer of 1925, the commission held hearings in Cody, Moran, and Jackson to discuss the future of the Jackson Hole–Teton country. The Forest Service, operator of Teton National Forest, wanted to retain exclusive control over the region, arguing that its multi-use approach to the conservation of the nation's resources made it the appropriate agency for governing the region. It could promote both recreational and commercial values, whereas the less flexible Park Service could promote only recreational values. In a commercially rich and extraordinarily scenic area, the Forest Service felt it could guarantee the best of two worlds. The Park Service knew better.

The Forest Service planned to license commercial lumbering operations on Jackson Lake, open several mines in northern Jackson Hole, and continue issuing grazing permits. A transfer of the forest to park status would have meant no private lumbering or mining operations and stricter limitations on grazing privileges. The Park Service, of course, advocated transfer. The commission voted three to two in favor of adding the Tetons and part of Jackson Hole to Yellowstone Park. Later, in order to secure a unanimous decision, the vote was reconsidered and only a portion of the Teton Range was approved for park status, the northern third of the range being omitted because of one unproved but potentially valuable asbestos claim on Berry Creek.[18]

Some Jackson Holers remained hostile to park extension in any form, others were content to go along with the co-ordinating commission's recommendation as long as this would be the last extension of Yellowstone Park. A few diehards opposed any kind of conservation effort. Many of the more influential citizens, although opposed to the in-clusion of Jackson Hole in an enlarged Yellowstone, favored the creation of a recreation area under some kind of govern-ment administration. A considerable segment of the latter group made its ideas known in a petition circulated by veteran ranchers Si Ferrin and Pierce Cunningham. Signed by ninety-seven property owners and sent to Casper, Wyo-ming, where the status of Jackson Hole was being debated publicly, the petition said in part:

> . . . we believe that the entire Jacksons Hole should be set aside as a recreational area, or should be admin-istered as a recreational area, through whatever agency, State or national, is considered best fitted to do it.
>
> . . . under the present administration of the public domain here, which is by the Forest Service, we are confronted by a policy which works to the detriment of stock raising without definitely turning over the country to wild life and recreation. By trying to do two things at once, with the same area, thereby trying to please those interested in stock and those interested in recreation, the Forest Service has succeeded only in making life miserable for all concerned.
>
> We have tried ranching, stock raising, and from our experience have become of the firm belief that this region will find its highest use as a playground. That in

this way it will become the greatest wealth-producing region of the State.

The destiny of Jacksons Hole is as a playground, typical of the West, for the education and enjoyment of the Nation as a whole. It is inevitable that it shall someday become such a region, and we favor a definite setting aside of the country at one time, instead of piecemeal, to its recreational purpose. Small extensions of recreational values and range restrictions only cause confusion and tend to squeeze us out, little by little from our business.[19]

Congress ignored the pleas for a national recreation area and concentrated instead on the co-ordinating commission's proposal to extend Yellowstone's boundaries. In March, 1926, a bill[20] incorporating all of the commission's recommendations was introduced in the Senate. Frank Gooding of Idaho proposed an amendment to eliminate the Bechler Meadows section of the original Yellowstone rectangle from the enlarged park so that Idaho interests could erect an irrigation project there. At Gooding's request, a Senate subcommittee convened in St. Anthony, Idaho, where the deteriorating farms and the pressing need for irrigated water could be inspected at first hand. Although the Park Service indicated a willingness to bargain, an agreement was not reached and the bill was never reported out of committee.[21]

CHAPTER SIXTEEN

ROCKEFELLER AND A NEW
NATIONAL PARK

By 1926 the effects of uncontrolled exploitation and irre-
sponsible bureacratic supervision had grown far worse. Dis-
playing very poor judgment, the Forest Service allowed a
telephone line to be stretched along the west side of the
Jenny Lake–Moran road, thereby impairing the motorist's
view of the Tetons. The Forest Service intended to open
parts of the valley to wealthy individuals for summer homes.
A dance hall and rows of tourist cabins were being erected
near Jenny Lake. Tumble-down gas stations and food
stands began to line the valley's roadways. As a grim example of what lay in store for the future, a billboard
advertising the Hollywood Cowboy's Home was placed on
Chester A. Goss's Elbo Ranch at the base of the Grand
Teton. With Congress hopelessly deadlocked on park extension and local conservationists unable to finance a

national recreation area, the onetime trappers' paradise of Jackson Hole seemed consigned to the dung heap of commercialism. Fortunately, however, the perseverance of Horace Albright and the generosity of an eastern philanthropist changed all that.

Through the years, Superintendent Albright had continued to work in his own indefatigable way for preservation of the Jackson Hole country. Each of his annual reports emphasized the urgency of annexing the Tetons. Whenever state officials, congressmen, editors, columnists, or leading sportsmen visited Yellowstone, he brought them south to Jackson Hole, where they could see for themselves the need for conservation. In 1926, philanthropist John D. Rockefeller, Jr., his wife, and their three younger sons vacationed in Yellowstone Park. Rockefeller had seen parts of Jackson Hole in 1924 and was anxious to inspect the valley more thoroughly, so Albright drove the Rockefellers south to the old Jackson Lake Lodge at Moran and, the next morning, on to the Bar BC and the JY. Along the way, they saw the disgraceful spread of architectural rubbish so close to the magnificent Tetons. Disgusted with the sight, Rockefeller asked Albright to furnish a map of the offensive properties and to estimate the cost of acquiring them. Later that day, the Rockefellers returned to Moran via the eastern side of Jackson Hole. When they paused at Hedrick's Point to gaze upon the magnificent panorama, Albright mentioned his dream, also shared by others, to save and restore the whole upper valley. He spoke of the meeting at Maud Noble's cabin three years earlier. The Rockefellers listened, but said nothing.

The following winter, Albright called on Rockefeller in New York to give him a map of the offending properties at the base of the Tetons and a list of estimated purchase prices prepared by Dick Winger. Rockefeller took one look at the map and remarked that it did not begin to cover what he had in mind. He said he was a man who believed in ideals and that Albright's dream of preserving all of Jackson Hole was one which deeply interested him. It was a wonderful surprise for Albright, who had come to New York hoping for a pledge of $250,000 and now found Rockefeller willing to commit himself to a purchasing program that might cost several million dollars. More maps and estimates were necessary to get the program under way. Albright promised to keep Rockefeller's name secret. Residents would demand more than their properties were worth if they knew that a man of Rockefeller's almost unlimited resources was trying to buy them out.[1]

To enable him to buy property in Jackson Hole while remaining anonymous, Rockefeller had his attorneys organize the Snake River Land Company, a Utah corporation with New York lawyer Vanderbilt Webb as president. Harold P. Fabian, a Salt Lake City law partner of Albright's classmate and close friend Beverly C. Clendenin, was retained as company attorney and vice president. Kenneth Chorley, an administrator of Rockefeller philanthropic interests, acted as liaison between Rockefeller and the company officials. Jackson Hole banker Robert Miller was hired as resident purchasing agent, much to the dismay of Dick Winger, who had expected that position. The choice of Miller was probably a tactical one. As bank president and leading citizen, he possessed a greater power of persuasion than ony other resident of the valley. His tacit threat of foreclosure was often enough to convince mortgaged landowners to sell. Furthermore, his many years in the valley enabled him to know the approximate worth of most properties.

Miller was never taken into the complete confidence of the Snake River Land Company officials. He was not told that John D. Rockefeller, Jr., was his ultimate employer, nor was he informed that Horace Albright had any connection with the purchasing scheme. Miller harbored a dislike for Albright dating back to the latter's earliest days in Yellowstone. As self-declared boss of the valley, Miller was jealous of any intrusion into his sphere of influence by his northern neighbor, and as a former Forest Service employee, he retained that bureau's distrust of the Park Service and its plans for expansion.[2]

Miller proved to be a problem child for the Snake River Land Company. He neglected private holdings on the more scenic western side of the valley with the excuse that their owners were demanding too high a price. He preferred to spend the company's money on ranches at the eastern side of the valley, where his bank held many mortgages and stood to gain from sale of the properties. He may also have discriminated among potential sellers; his enemies claimed that he offered to buy their properties only at unfairly low prices.[3]

In 1928, when Congress again took up the co-ordinating commission's 1925 recommendations for annexation of the Tetons, Miller suspected some secret connection between the park extension efforts and his employer's purchasing scheme. Company officials tried to allay his suspicions. Vanderbilt Webb wrote:

> I have noted the reference in your letter to the Yellowstone National Park extension bills which have been introduced at Washington. This is the first I have heard of these bills, and I do not know who is responsible for them. Neither I nor my clients have had any-

thing to do with them, and they are in no way connected with our plan.[4]

Harold Fabian added:

You can rest assured and can honestly assure others
that our project is entirely independent from the new
park, and has nothing whatever to do with it, although
I can't see just what difference it should make anyway
to an individual whose land we are buying what it is
being bought for, provided we are willing to pay a price
for it.[5]

Technically, there was no connection between the purchasing program and the park extension schemes, but there was
considerable behind-the-scenes co-operation between the
Park Service and the land company. Had Miller known of
it, he might have suspected that the Park Service would be
the ultimate benefactor of his purchases. Not one to further
the dreams of his avowed enemy, Horace Albright, Miller
would later resign upon learning of Albright's close relationship with the company. Dick Winger, who helped negotiate
purchases from his friends on the west side of the Snake,
would succeed Miller.

The proposed legislation which aroused Miller's suspicions brought a Senate subcommittee to Jackson Hole in
July, 1928. Open hearings were held in the hall above Bruce
Porter's drugstore in Jackson and the following day at the
JY Ranch to consider the advisability of enlarging Yellowstone Park or creating a separate Teton National Park.[6]
Seventy-six of the seventy-seven townspeople at the Jackson
gathering were in favor of a Teton park. The JY meeting
was called at the insistence of State Senator Will Deloney
and other park opponents who had missed the Jackson

meeting because of a time mixup. Wyoming's U.S. Senator John B. Kendrick was extremely effective in persuading the JY audience to affirm the vote taken in Jackson. The dude ranchers present were assured that the proposed legislation would be amended to prohibit the construction of hotels, new roads, and new permanent camps in the Teton park.

Several years later, Senator Kendrick claimed that his support for the park proposal had been given in exchange for Albright's promise that the Park Service would never ask to expand Teton National Park.[7] Albright, appointed director of the Park Service in 1929, denied having made such a promise and claimed that his ambition to acquire Jackson Hole for the Park Service was well known. The most that he may have promised was that Yellowstone Park would not be extended into the valley. He recalled that at the close of the JY meeting, Will Deloney hooked him by the arm and said, "Well, Albright, now that you've got the park, I suppose you'll try to get the whole valley." Albright replied that the Park Service was glad to get a foothold and would certainly push for expansion. Senator Kendrick may not have known that part of this effort would be accomplished through a private land company dedicated to conservation, but he certainly knew of the company's recent purchases, for Will Deloney had mentioned them in his presence at the JY meeting. The Senator was badly mistaken if he thought the Park Service would not try to acquire at least some of the Snake River Land Company's property.[8]

At any rate, Kendrick's bill[9] creating Grand Teton National Park passed Congress on February 26, 1929. The park embraced the east slope of the Teton Range from Webb Canyon south to Granite Canyon and a narrow strip of the valley floor along the base of the range. The beautiful piedmont lakes at the foot of the Tetons were also included, except for Jackson Lake, which remained under Bureau of Reclamation administration. The new addition comprised a nearly solid block of federal lands requiring only a simple transfer from Forest Service to Park Service jurisdiction.

One of the earliest achievements it inspired was the renovation of near-by Jackson Lake. To finance the project, the Park Service convinced Congress to appropriate $50,000 and to set aside $50,000 from the Reclamation Bureau's Minidoka Project Funds. The sums were pooled and a contract was let to clear debris from the shoreline. The Civilian Conservation Corps spent several summers on the job.[10]

CHAPTER SEVENTEEN

BITTER CONTROVERSY

While the Park Service worked to save the Tetons, a parallel effort was being conducted by the Snake River Land Company to protect Jackson Hole, which, by virtue of its flatness, made the jagged Tetons so spectacular and so worth saving. The efforts of each organization complemented those of the other. If the Tetons had been left open to commercial abuse, little reason would have remained for cleaning up the adjacent valley. Had the Snake River Land Company not blocked the spread of commercialism on the valley floor, the Park Service's preservation of the Tetons would have been wasted for all those people who would view the mountains from below.

The officers of the Snake River Land Company occupied a rather delicate position in this scheme. They hoped to complete Rockefeller's land acquisition program while antagonizing as little of the government and local populace as possible—quite an undertaking considering the number of interested groups holding variant views on the subject.[1] One such group was the Elk Commission, appointed by the President's Committee on Outdoor Recreation. In 1927, Representative Charles E. Winter introduced a bill recommending the addition of 12,000 acres to the National Elk Refuge north of Jackson. The bill failed, but Winter was able to get Congress to accept the donation of a small adjacent parcel which the Izaak Walton League had acquired in 1925. The Elk Commission met in 1927 and endorsed Winter's original recommendations for enlargement.[2] The commission reconvened in 1929 because the Snake River Land Company was buying properties which the commission had earmarked for an enlarged elk refuge.[3] After assuring the commission that its concern for the elk was shared by them, the land company officials promised an eventual donation of the tracts in question to the elk refuge.[4]

The Snake River Land Company encountered other groups with their own ideas on how the firm should ultimately dispose of its purchases. The Wyoming Game Commission did not want an enlarged federal elk refuge, nor did it want the National Park Service to acquire the company's holdings on the east side of the Snake. Both the Park Service and the refuge administration would prohibit hunting and foster overpopulation of the elk. Nor did the Game Commission consider the Forest Service an acceptable alternative, for the latter could not be trusted to keep sheep off the summer elk range. The commission preferred a state game refuge in part of the valley and seasonal hunting in

181

the rest. Many Wyoming hunters supported the commission, which, unlike certain other state agencies, had an admirable conservation record.

The U.S. Forest Service believed that commercial and recreational uses were compatible and that if the land company's purchases were turned over to it, the use of the valley's resources would be maximized. Because the Forest Service held considerable prestige in local political circles, its views were a force to be reckoned with.[5] The Park Service, of course, expected to get the lion's share of the Snake River Land Company's properties. Grand Teton Superintendent Sam Woodring co-operated closely with the firm, and Director Albright kept in constant communication with company officials and local supporters of park expansion.[6] Many local inhabitants still adhered to the concept of a national recreational area, first broached at Maud Noble's cabin in 1923. State Senator Will Deloney adopted the idea and made an impressive presentation of it to the Special Senate Committee on Wildlife Resources holding hearings in Jackson Hole.[7]

In an effort to reconcile some of the opposing factions without abandoning Rockefeller's ultimate objectives, Snake River Land Company Vice President Harold Fabian suggested[8] that land west of the Snake be added to Grand Teton Park and land east of the Snake be administered by the Biological Survey, partly as a preserve and partly as open hunting ground. Although Fabian's plan was a judicious compromise and might have eliminated ground for future discontent, it was not approved by John D. Rockefeller, Jr. The wealthy New Yorker had grown fond of Horace Albright and put more faith in Albright's Park Service than in any other federal or state agency. When the appropriate time for donation should arrive, Rockefeller intended to entrust the Park Service with the bulk of his properties on both sides of the river. The elk refuge would receive the remainder.

As Rockefeller's intentions became known, more fuel was added to the fires of controversy. Among the settlers of Jackson Hole, the conflict over the destiny of their valley degenerated into a bitter mountain feud. According to Olaus J. Murie, the well-known naturalist who lived in Jackson Hole from 1927 until his death in 1963, the controversy

> went beyond the state of reasoning for or against a plan; it had become a personal battle, a case of loyalty to one side or to the other . . . .
>
> Card parties, dinner parties had their embarrassments if certain ones prominent on "the other side" were present. In some inexplicable way an atmosphere was created in which one felt inhibited from even mentioning the subject. There was no such thing as getting together and talking it over.[9]

The Jackson Lions Club passed several resolutions against park extension.[10] On one occasion, Rockefeller reportedly appeared before the club in an attempt to change its members' views.[11] The Jackson Hole Commercial Club, on the other hand, applauded Rockefeller's efforts and advocated extension of Grand Teton National Park as far south as Jackson so that the town's businessmen could benefit from the growing tourist trade. The long-established *Jackson's Hole Courier* took a pro-park line, but it soon had a competitor in the bitterly anti-park *Grand Teton*. In its little more than two years' existence, the *Grand Teton* conducted what Leslie A. Miller, Wyoming's pro-park Democratic governor and later trustee for the Rockefeller interests, described as a "virulent, vicious, and indecent campaign" against park extension. The rivalry between the two newspapers took on a partisan political flavor spiced with personal animosity.[12]

Some of the most outspoken opponents of park extension were cattlemen. Despite Washington's assurance that the Park Service was empowered to permit grazing on park property, the ranchers feared these privileges would be denied if Grand Teton were extended to include Rockefeller's purchases and adjacent Forest Service lands. In opposing extension, the ranchmen and those who agreed with them drew upon two related strands of frontier thought: the pioneer's hatred of outside interference (in this case, the Park Service) and the rugged individualist's disdain for men of inherited wealth (such as John D. Rockefeller, Jr.).

The first of these traditional frontier attitudes had been in evidence in Jackson Hole since the federal government first began protecting forested areas south of Yellowstone Park in the 1890's. Federal control over grazing privileges in the timber reserves and national forests had irked local stockmen from its incepton. In 1903, after visiting Teton Forest Reserve, journalist Frederic Irland could report a growing sense of alienation among the ranchers, characterized by a distrust of central government and an almost class-oriented fear of the wealth behind that government:

> It is the impression of a great many people in Wyoming that the government of the United States is acting as a cat's-paw for the eastern sportsmen's league that avowedly wishes to drive the cattle from the mountains and the settlers from their homes. They fear a variation of the black page of English history when the rich and powerful confiscated the homes of

Climbers on pinnacle near Symmetry Spire,
Grand Teton National Park

COURTESY NATIONAL PARK SERVICE
PHOTOGRAPH BY HERB POWNALL

Climber's cairn on Peak 10552, southeast of Static Peak

Jackson Hole Ski Area, Teton Village, with lodges and parking
facilities at the base

Aerial tramway at Jackson Hole Ski Area

Rendezvous Bowl, Jackson Hole Ski Area

Skiing the deep powder at Jackson Hole Ski Area

Buffalo feeding on wildlife range, Grand Teton National Park

COURTESY NATIONAL PARK SERVICE

PHOTOGRAPH BY BRYAN HARRY

View up Death Canyon toward Mount Bannon

the lowly to make hunting parks for the amusement
of the great.[13]

The Snake River Land Company, of course, did not intend
to create hunting parks for the wealthy. Rockefeller's grand
design was to preserve the valley for all people. He and
the advocates of park expansion recognized that with the
return of economic prosperity and the mass distribution of
automobiles, a national park vacation would be possible for
nearly every class of Americans.

By 1933, the Snake River Land Company had contracted
to buy properties on both sides of Jackson Hole totaling
35,310 acres and costing $1,400,310, or an average of $39
per acre. The prices paid were often in excess of what the
properties were worth. For land appraised by the state of
Wyoming at $521,037, the company offered $1,316,672.
Inflated asking prices on some properties were unavoidable
after the public disclosure in 1930 that a Rockefeller was the
land company's chief stockholder.[14]

Some of the more noteworthy Rockefeller purchases
were Si Ferrin's Elk Ranch between Spread Creek and
Buffalo River, Pierce Cunningham's Spread Creek outfit,
the Noble and Menor properties at Moose, Ben Sheffield's
Moran layout, and Chester Goss's Elbo Ranch on Taggart
Creek. Several dude ranches were also purchased and then
leased back to their former owners on term- or lifetime-
tenancy bases. Dude ranching was thought by the Rockefeller interests to be worth preserving, if only on a somewhat
limited scale.

When the Snake River Land Company bought a property, the buildings on it were either repaired, moved, or
dismantled. Si Ferrin's ranch buildings, situated on the
east side of the valley away from the Tetons, did not inter-

fere with the tourist's view of the mountains and were retained and renovated. On the other hand, the offensive rodeo ground which had grown up around the Elbo Ranch at the base of the Tetons was completely destroyed. Race track, bucking shoots, stables, grandstand, billboard, hot-dog stands, and barbed-wire fences were taken down and the area they occupied returned to sagebrush. The entire town of Moran, with its extensive but rather ramshackle guest facilities, would have been demolished but for the valley's shortage of tourist accommodations.

The Teton Lodge Company was organized to continue tourist operations at Moran until more scenic accommodations could be built there or elsewhere. The Snake River Land Company granted the lodge firm a ten-year lease on the Moran buildings, plus the right to operate remodeled gas stations and stores at Moose and Jenny Lake. The stock of the Teton Lodge Company was owned by Teton Investment Company, which was also a holding concern for two other corporations: Teton Transportation Company, which ran the Moran-Victor stage line, and Jackson Lake Lodge, Inc. The last-named corporation operated Jackson Lake Lodge, a former Amoretti Chain inn overlooking Jackson Lake from the bluff just north of Moran. Built in 1922, the lodge has been replaced by a modern motor hotel of the same name. None of the corporations, except Snake River Land Company, was owned by John D. Rockefeller, Jr., but through his policy of leasing land and lending capital to them, he maintained considerable control over their activities.[15]

Rockefeller's initial anonymity in the purchasing program and the secrecy which characterized his negotiations with official Washington gave rise to a number of rumors and accusations, usually unfounded. The opponents of park extension leveled charges of collusion, conflict of interest, misrepresentation of intentions, and unconscionable bargaining against Rockefeller and the Park Service. Partly in response to these charges and partly because of outrage in some quarters over recent public-land withdrawals, a subcommittee of the Senate Public Lands Committee held hearings in Jackson from August 7 to 10, 1933.[16] The charge that Rockefeller was purchasing land to make money was dismissed as frivolous. He could not make a profit from the land itself, since he intended to give it away. The concession companies which he directly or indirectly controlled were fortunate if they broke even. Furthermore, he had encouraged Wyoming citizens to buy stock and assume executive positions in the companies. In this way, he had done much to disprove the contention that outsiders were trying to take over the valley. The subcommittee was shown that ranchers had not been driven from their homes, but that the land company had been generous, sometimes exceedingly so, in its offers and that the ranchers had been free to accept or reject them. No one had been forced to sell.

An accusation that Horace Albright was financially interested in the Rockefeller enterprise was not substantiated. His interest lay in conservation and the achievement of Park Service ideals. He may have been guilty of evasion and perhaps deception, but such practices were necessary if the difficult job of saving Jackson Hole from commercial abuse was to be successful. Albright doubted that any organization except one completely dedicated to conservation and backed by national power could do the job. His Park Service was the only organization which fit the bill.

In a utopian political scheme, collusion between a private land-buying outfit and a government bureau, such as the Park Service, would, of course, be unethical. But in the real world, when the issue is as paramount as conservation and the problems involved cannot be solved entirely in the open, secret co-operation between interested public and private groups is beneficial and is to be expected. In a system of checks and balances, it is for other branches of the government to assure that the bureaucracy does not abuse this privilege to deal in secret. With one exception, the subcommittee of the Senate Public Lands Committee absolved the Park Service and the Snake River Land Company. That one exception concerned the application of Albert W. Gabbey for a stockraising addition to his homestead near Jenny Lake. In its zeal to block commercial expansion around the lake, the Park Service had prevailed upon the Geological Survey to delay consideration of Gabbey's application and ultimately to reject it on the ground that the land was unfit for stockraising. The Park Service suspected that Gabbey intended to build tourist cottages. Meanwhile, the tract in question was ordered withdrawn from entry. The Senate subcommittee apparently concluded that the Park Service had improperly interfered with Gabbey's application and that he should be given a second chance.[17]

Following the subcommittee's hearings, Congress attempted to deal with the future of Rockefeller's holdings and other problems aired at the hearings. Senator Robert D. Carey of Wyoming offered a bill[18] to expand Grand Teton National Park to include the northern Tetons, Jackson Lake, Emma Matilda and Two Ocean lakes, much of the Buffalo River drainage, part of Phelps Lake, and all of Jackson Hole on the east side of the Snake as far south as Jackson, including the elk refuge. There was to be a six-mile-wide strip of national forest separating Yellowstone and Grand Teton parks. The Biological Survey would administer the east side of the park, the Park Service the west. Cattle rights-of-way were to be protected. Existing summer-home and commercial leases would be continued for at least twenty-five and ten years, respectively, with lessees to be reimbursed for past improvements. Teton County and the Jackson Hole school districts were to be compensated for tax losses during the next ten years based on a full assessment and the following ten years at an annually declining rate of 10 per cent. In addition, the secretary of the Interior was directed to issue a patent in fee to Albert W. Gabbey for his disputed stockraising entry.

Senator Carey's bill passed the Senate. The House Public Lands Committee reported the measure favorably on the last day of the session, but with an amendment requested by the Bureau of the Budget requiring that tax-loss compensation be furnished through some means other than federal funds.[19] Congress adjourned the same day without further opportunity to act on the bill. In the next session of Congress, Senator Carey and his Wyoming colleague, Senator Joseph C. O'Mahoney, introduced a piece of legislation[20] similar to Carey's first bill except that it excluded Jackson, Emma Matilda, and Two Ocean lakes and the land north of the Buffalo and set aside the existing elk refuge as Jackson Hole National Game Refuge. Once again the budget director reacted unfavorably to the tax-compensation provision, and the measure never got out of committee. In 1938, the Park Service drafted a park-extension bill which would have enlarged Grand Teton Park to its present size.[21] A Senate subcommittee held hearings in Jackson concerning the proposal but made no recommendation.[22]

Congress' frequent insistence on considering the issue of park extension and its accompanying inability to act decisively on the matter created several unfortunate side effects. Local residents, thinking they would soon lose their properties by condemnation according to the law of eminent domain, hesitated to improve their land for fear their efforts would come to naught. Community projects had to be delayed until the future became more certain. A badly needed high school on Mormon Row (Jackson High School being fifteen miles away) was not built because taxpayers were unwilling to finance such an expensive project when it seemed likely their school district would, in the near future, lose its ability to maintain a new school. Rockefeller had bought many properties in the Mormon Row school district, and if these were to be turned over to the federal government with no stipulation for future tax payment, then the few remaining farmers would have shouldered the entire financial burden of operating a new school. Jackson Hole's economy had deteriorated initially because of the decline in the tourist business during the Great Depression. It grew more stagnant the longer the uncertainty of park extension hung over the valley.[23]

CHAPTER EIGHTEEN

JACKSON HOLE NATIONAL MONUMENT

For John D. Rockefeller, Jr., the failure of Congress to extend Grand Teton National Park was particularly discouraging. He hoped to turn his land over to the Park Service in the mid-1930's, but before doing so, he wanted to be sure that Congress would not simply reopen it for settlement once title had been transferred. Because of fluctuating levels in lobbyist pressure from conservationists and cattlemen, the mood of Congress throughout the 1930's was highly unpredictable. Rockefeller did not know how Congress would react to his gift, once officially made. Then, in the early 1940's, after consolidating his interests into Jackson Hole Preserve, Inc., he began to grow restless. For nearly ten years he had shouldered a large tax burden while waiting for signs from Washington that the time had arrived for his lands to be donated. Taxes were higher than ever before, and he was becoming ever more impatient. He decided to apply some personal pressure on key government personnel.

In 1942, Rockefeller wrote Secretary of the Interior Harold L. Ickes that if the government did not immediately accept his long-standing offer of land in Jackson Hole, he would dispose of his properties on the open market.[1] Implicit in Rockefeller's ultimatum was the threat of revived commercialism in Jackson Hole. Wishing to avoid at all costs the repetition of past abuses in the valley and knowing that immediate congressional approval of any park-extension scheme would be unlikely, Ickes was forced to resort to a normally undesirable tactic: executive fiat. He drew up a proclamation setting aside 221,610 acres of land in Jackson Hole, including almost all of Rockefeller's property, as a national monument and sent the proclamation to President Franklin D. Roosevelt for his approval. According to the 1906 Antiquities Act, the President could create national monuments by executive order. National parks had to be created by legislative action. President Theodore Roosevelt had acted under the provisions of the Antiquities Act when he established the first national monument at Devil's Tower, Wyoming.[2]

On March 15, 1943, Roosevelt signed Ickes' proclamation creating Jackson Hole National Monument. The press announcement of the President's action stunned the people of Jackson Hole. They knew nothing of Rockefeller's ultimatum and did not understand why Ickes and Roosevelt acted so abruptly and arbitrarily without consulting the people's elected state and national representatives. All of the settlers' past grievances with the federal government came sharply into focus. The traditional fear of outside interference, which had long typified the valley's attitude toward external government, now seemed justified. To complicate matters, most of Jackson Hole's voters were Republicans, inclined to believe the worst about the national Democratic administration.

The state government of Wyoming was appalled at Roosevelt's action and considered it a direct attack on the territorial integrity of the state. Because the proclamation contained no allowance for federal refunding of lost state and county tax dollars, it was also seen as an attack on Wyoming's financial solvency. Governor Lester C. Hunt pleaded with the President to withdraw the proclamation, but Roosevelt remained unmoved.[3]

Wyoming brought suit against the federal government, in the person of Paul R. Franke, superintendent of Grand Teton National Park and chief administrator of adjoining Jackson Hole National Monument. On February 10, 1945, U.S. District Judge T. Blake Kennedy decided generally in favor of the defendant and directed dismissal of the suit. Judge Kennedy described the case as "a controversy between the legislative and executive branches of the Government in which . . . the court cannot interefere." He added:

Undoubtedly great hardship and a substantial amount of injustice will be done to the State and her citizens if the executive department carries out its threatened program, but if the Congress presumes to delegate its inherent authority to executive departments which exercise acquisitive proclivities not actually intended, the burden is on the Congress to pass such remedial legislation as may obviate any injustice brought about, as the power and control over the disposition of Government lands inherently rests in its legislative branch.[4]

Congress, of course, already recognized its duty to resolve the problem. Representative Frank Barrett of Wyoming introduced a bill[5] to abolish the monument. Both houses passed Barrett's measure, but President Roosevelt killed the bill with a pocket veto.[6] Meanwhile, Representative J. Hardin Peterson of Florida introduced several pro-monument bills[7] providing for payments to Wyoming as compensation for tax losses. The proposals, which also guaranteed cattle rights-of-way over federal lands within the monument, were never passed by Congress.[8]

Opponents were not successful in further efforts to abolish Jackson Hole National Monument, but they did manage to hinder its administration. The Interior Department Appropriation Act for Fiscal Year 1945 carried the provision, first made in the act of the previous year at the insistence of Senator O'Mahoney, that no department funds would be available for any new administrative function or regulations which might be occasioned through the establishment of Jackson Hole National Monument. This provision effectively blocked the administration, protection, and maintenance of the area as a national monument per se. It could be governed only according to public-land regulations in force prior to its establishment.[9]

The dispute over Jackson Hole National Monument created a great stir in the nation's press. Not many newspapers outside Wyoming doubted the desirability of including the valley's scenic flatlands in the national park and monument system. But, at the same time, few editorials could defend the arbitrary manner in which the monument had been established. Roosevelt's proclamation smacked of the same apparent insensitivity to popular opinion and disrespect toward the other branches of government which had characterized his earlier scheme to pack the U.S. Supreme Court.

Much of the criticism of Roosevelt, however, was uninformed and unjustified. Columnist Westbrook Pegler, conveniently forgetting that nearly every chief executive since Theodore Roosevelt had created national monuments, likened the proclamation to Hitler's *Anschluss*. Others asserted that the government was dragging settlers from their homes, leaving cattle to starve. One incensed senator referred to the President's action as "a foul, sneaking Pearl Harbor blow." In a headline-grabbing stunt, western movie actor Wallace Beery, the lessee of a summer-home site on Jackson Lake, led a defiant band of ranchers and cattle across monument boundaries to protest Roosevelt's decision. The ranchers apparently did not know that their rights-of-way through the monument were unaffected by the proclamation.[10]

For the remainder of the 1940's, proposals to abolish Jackson Hole National Monument or to appropriate funds for it were battered around in Congress and in the press, but no final decision was forthcoming. Conservation groups conducted vigorous propaganda campaigns against its abolition. The forces of commercialism and states' rights carried on equally vigorous campaigns in favor of such action. A number of the West's biggest cattlemen lobbied intensively for abolition. They had no great interest in Jackson Hole as such, but they felt that any well-publicized defeat of conservation forces would help pave the way for a few large, influential stockmen to gain complete control over the vast unoccupied public lands remaining in the West.

By 1950, however, conservationists were emerging victorious. The bitterness over the arbitrary nature of Roosevelt's proclamation had faded, and Congress was able to investigate the issue with greater emotional detachment and a sense of historical perspective. In the light of calm rationality, it resolved the controversy by enlarging Grand Teton National Park to include Jackson Hole National

Monument. A pair of once bitter opponents of the monument, Senators O'Mahoney and Hunt of Wyoming, introduced the enlarging measure,[11] and on September 14, 1950, President Harry S Truman affixed his signature to the act establishing a new Grand Teton National Park. Deeds to Rockefeller lands within the former national monument had been officially presented to the government nine months before. The 1950 act provided that existing leases would continue for twenty-five years and thereafter during the life of the lessee and the lives of his heirs, successors, and assigns if they were members of the lessee's immediate family before the act was passed.[12]

The enlargement of Grand Teton National Park meant that only 4 per cent of what would normally be taxable property in Teton County was available for taxation. The 1950 act required the Park Service to compensate the local government for its loss of tax revenue by paying the equivalent of a full tax assessment for an initial ten-year period. The payments, which were to be financed from the park's visitor fees, would be reduced 5 per cent each year during a second ten-year period. By 1970, payments to Teton County would cease. The reasoning behind the reduction in payments was that park expansion and accompanying publicity would stimulate tourism, an industry composed of taxable business which would themselves contribute to the county government's total revenue.[13]

CHAPTER NINETEEN

GRAND TETON NATIONAL PARK AND JACKSON HOLE TODAY

Today Grand Teton National Park is one of the most popular attractions in the entire national park system. Motorists who drive by the Tetons on their way to Yellowstone are amazed at the spectacular beauty of the younger park. Many return to Jackson Hole the next summer to spend an entire vacation. Since 1963, Grand Teton National Park has attracted more visitors annually than its northern neighbor. In 1965, more than 2,500,000 people went to Grand Teton, whereas only slightly more than 2,000,000 visited Yellowstone. During the same year, Teton National Forest recorded 469,500 recreation visits.[1]

The park, the forest, and the rest of Jackson Hole offer outstanding recreational opportunities for the visitor: hiking, fishing, golfing, swimming, boating, water skiing, horseback riding, and mountain climbing in the summer;

205

hunting, skiing, cutter racing (featuring horse-drawn sleds), and snowmobiling in the winter; and photography the year round. Wildlife is plentiful along the Snake River bottomlands, elk can be seen in the National Elk Refuge, and buffalo graze on the Jackson Hole Wildlife Range, a gift from Laurance S. Rockefeller (son of John D., Jr.) and the New York Zoological Society.

For the history buff, the Rockefeller interests have rebuilt Menor's Ferry at Moose and the Park Service has reconstructed the so-called Horse Thieves' Barn on the Pierce Cunningham homestead. It is unfortunate, though, that the Park Service has not preserved more old homesteads to illustrate frontier life in the age of settlement. The park operates several visitor centers and two museums, one dealing with the history of mountain climbing in the Tetons and the other concerning the fur trade. The town of Jackson has preserved authentic items from the days of trappers, outlaws, and settlers in its Jackson Hole Museum.

The Forest Service maintains a geological observation area at the Gros Ventre slide, where in 1925 tons of rock slid off Sheep Mountain, damming the Gros Ventre River below. Rupture of the dam by high water in 1927 resulted in the death of six people and the total destruction of the village of Kelly, which has since been partially rebuilt. At the time of the catastrophe, Kelly was nearly as populous as Jackson. Had the unfortunate village not been so devastated by the flood waters, it, instead of Jackson, might have become the central metropolis of the valley.[2]

For those with a true spirit of adventure, the Tetons offer some of the best mountain climbing in North America. The metamorphosed rock is "clean"—that is, holds together well and is relatively free of slides. The twisted schists and gneisses provide cracks and ledges where climbers can get foot and hand holds and insert pitons. Despite the height and steepness of some portions of the Tetons, beginners have been known to reach the summit of the Grand Teton after only a few days of practice and instruction. Nearly all routes have been rated in difficulty so that the climber can decide beforehand which routes are suited to his abilities. A combined mountaineering school and guide service is maintained at Jenny Lake, and climbing equipment can be purchased at several stores in Jackson. In the Tetons, the emphasis is on safety. All climbers must register at the Jenny Lake Ranger Station, listing their intended route, expected time of departure and return, and the number in their party. No solo climbing is allowed. Registration is imperative so that rescue efforts, if needed, can be undertaken at the earliest possible moment.

Like any dangerous sport, mountain climbing in the Tetons has had its share of tragedies. Some climbers have foolishly removed their safety ropes in mid-climb, lost their balance, and tumbled to their deaths. Others have gone into the mountains with ropes frayed or stretched from previous climbs. When one of these ill-equipped climbers slips (not an unusual occurrence) and falls the length of his weakened rope, it may break, sending him hurtling toward the rocks far below. To bring out the bodies of the injured and the dead, the Park Service operates a rescue service, whose members' daring and resourcefulness can hardly be matched.

Perhaps the most spectacular rescue in the Tetons thus far was conducted in late July, 1962. Seven men and three women, ranging in age from eighteen to sixty-five, were ascending the Grand Teton when an unusually severe storm of ice and snow stranded them on a ledge. They had failed to register at Jenny Lake; consequently, rescue operations did not begin until their companions in the valley reported them missing. Much of the rescue operation took place at night, the rescuers wearing miners' headlamps to aid in the search. When help reached the stricken group, one person had died and others had become hysterical from forty-eight hours' exposure to cold and moisture. One of the climbers thought the rescuers were "one-eyed devils" who had come to pull them down into hell. He resisted violently and raced back up the mountain until one of the rescuers subdued him with a blow on the head. Too numb to descend on their own, the climbers were lowered in canvas bags. Miraculously, the nine survivors and their valiant rescuers survived the harrowing descent. Helicopters landing on the saddle between the Grand and Middle Tetons flew the most seriously injured to a hospital. The lone victim was buried on the snowfield where he died.[3]

Much of Jackson Hole's tourist appeal is based on its reputation as a former hideout for highwaymen, cattle rustlers, and horse thieves. Playing the western outlaw theme to the hilt, local businessmen have placed billboards on Hoback Rim and Teton Pass which proclaim to the incoming tourist: "Howdy stranger, yonder is Jackson Hole, the last of the Old West!" Every summer evening, crowds of visitors gather on the main intersection at Jackson to see some of the local citizenry re-enact an episode in frontier justice. Clover the Killer is apprehended by the Cache Creek Posse for robbing a stagecoach; he is to be hanged from an elkhorn arch. At the last moment, Clover is given a chance to die a nobler death—in a shoot out with the marshal. Members of Clover's gang suddenly appear from behind the false fronts of several stores but are gunned down in a fusillade of fire (from blank cartridges, of course) which also kills Clover. In contrast to its outlaw image,

Jackson Hole offers the Pink Garter and Diamond Lil theaters, a fine arts festival, several painting studios, and the Laubin Indian Dances, which provide residents and tourists alike with a cultural refinement unavailable to Clover the Killer and his ilk.

Accommodations in the valley include guest ranches (updated dude ranches), housekeeping cabins, Jackson's hotel and motels, the recently expanded Signal Mountain Lodge, sprawling Jackson Lake Lodge, exclusive Jenny Lake Lodge, and things similar. Most of the concessions within the national park are operated by the Rockefeller interests—Grand Teton Lodge Company and Jackson Hole Preserve, Inc.—on a non-profit basis. The Park Service and the Forest Service maintain seventeen campgrounds, varying from the primitive tent-and-sleeping bag variety to the modern trailer village. Paved Jackson Hole Highway, its spur roads, and Jackson Hole Airport help to solve the region's inherent transportation difficulties. Wyoming Highway Department crews keep the Hoback, Snake River, Togwotee, and Teton Pass routes clear of snow and rock during the winter. In the future, the Park Service may operate the highway north into Yellowstone on a full-time basis.

In spite of—and partially because of—all these modern conveniences, the conflict between commercialization and conservation continues in Jackson Hole. The town of Jackson is developing into a haven of commercial enterprise. Its neon-lighted bars and night clubs remind one of a miniature Hollywood or Las Vegas. Dirt roads have been replaced by paved thoroughfares. Souvenir shops with garish displays line the streets. The town's Old West spirit is being buried in a graveyard of service stations and "gas for less" signs. Where settlers were once content to eke out a living and enjoy twelve months of clean air and charming scenery each and every year, most residents today are caught up in a three-month, hell-bent pursuit of the almighty dollar. In a modern world where wealth, not happiness, seems to be the watchword, the sentiments of Jackson's businessmen can be understood, though hardly condoned.[4]

The appearance of ski resorts in the valley marks the advent of a new form of commercialism. Since its founding in 1946, Snow King Mountain south of Jackson has remained a small-scale operation. But the relatively recent (1965) Jackson Hole Ski Area, on the Tetons above Teton Village, promises to become one of the largest ski complexes in North America. Jackson Hole has always needed a year-round source of income. Because skiing provides this sorely needed wintertime equivalent of the tourist business, the building of ski slopes in Jackson Hole is a welcome development. But ski operations, with their man-made lifts, tramways, and base lodges, tend to mar the landscape. Not much can be done to beautify lifts or trams, but if ski lodge architecture is kept simple, tasteful, and in accordance with the general Old West theme of the valley, the effect on Jackson Hole's scenery will not be disruptive. As long as commercial skiing enterprises are prohibited on the more spectacular portions of the Teton Range within Grand Teton National Park, the threat to aesthetics can be held to a minimum.

Another form of commercialism, the filming of movies and television programs, is commonplace in Jackson Hole. The film companies must get Park Service permission before erecting their sets and are required to return the land to its natural state when they are finished. This form of commercialism, therefore, is rarely harmful and is economically beneficial. Funds expended by producers and casts contribute directly to the community's welfare, and publicity from the films provides indirect benefits. Among those who demonstrated their acting talents in the shadow of the Tetons were Tom Mix in *The Three Bad Men* (1925), John Wayne in *The Big Trail* (1929), and Wallace Beery in *Wyoming* (1939) and *Bad Bascomb* (1945).

In the early 1950's, Hollywood invaded Jackson Hole in force, and at one time three movie companies were shooting there simultaneously. *Jubal*, starring Glenn Ford, was filmed on the Triangle X Ranch. Across the valley on the Snake River, Kirk Douglas was appearing in *The Big Sky*, while only a few miles away Alan Ladd was doing *Shane*. Henry Fonda and Maureen O'Hara spent several weeks in the valley for *Spencer's Mountain* (1964). The most popular of canine stars romped across Jackson Hole's photogenic landscape for *Son of Lassie* in 1942. Other movies included *Nanette of the North* (1921), *The Cowboy and the Lady* (1922), and *Far Horizons* (1954). During the summer of 1966, a television series, *The Monroes*, was filmed on location in Jackson Hole.[5]

A few commercial threats are still found within or near the boundaries of Grand Teton National Park and Teton National Forest. Cattle ranching will probably always pose a potential threat. One rancher just outside park lines has marred the landscape by erecting a wall of automobile frames to prevent Buffalo River from washing away a section of embankment adjoining his property. At this writing, cattlemen are guaranteed grazing rights on national forest land and driving rights through Park Service property. Three prosperous ranchers have managed to obtain special grazing privileges on government-owned Elk Ranch. There, the American taxpayer is furnishing them with expensive irrigation water at absurdly low prices. If inequitable situations like this one and disconcerting scenes like the automobile junk pile along Buffalo River are eliminated and if government officials remain firm and fair in their decisions concerning grazing practices, cattle ranching and the U.S. government will be able to coexist peacefully in the future. The Forest Service guards against commercial abuses perpetrated by lumbering and mining firms licensed to operate within national forest borders. Oil companies are required to restore all Forest Service drilling sites to their natural state.

Some of the most unfortunate challenges to the natural beauty of Jackson Hole come from the governmental agencies assigned to protect that beauty. Paved roads, parking lots, garbage dumps, and telephone lines, created by the Park Service and the Forest Service, clearly detract from the wildness and splendor of the valley. But these detractions have come about out of necessity; they result from the demands of an expanding tourist population which desires comfortable facilities and certain conveniences of home.

Sometimes the government's seemingly unconservationist actions are caused not by necessity, but by poor planning. The Park Service's all-too-modern employee homes and maintenance buildings at Moose could have been constructed in a more traditional western style and placed in a more secluded setting, perhaps at Beaver Creek. Tourists traveling through one of the most scenic rural valleys in the world do not like to be reminded of modern suburban living at its ugliest.

The conflict between conservation and commercialization will probably continue forever in Jackson Hole. Because of efforts by the Rockefellers, the Park Service, and conservation-minded settlers, however, the valley's essential loveliness has been preserved for all time. The main battle has been won; only minor skirmishes remain to be fought.

The victory of Jackson Hole's conservationists is evidence of the vast change that has occurred in American attitudes and ideals since the beginning of the twentieth century. In 1901, the reigning doctrine of laissez-faire individualism protected commercial interests from the infant forces of conservation, but as the century progressed, the gradually more popular concept of social ownership began to undermine the strength of commercial dogma. Today, the conservationists' philosophy, the very essence of which advocates collective control of the nation's natural resources for the common good, is gaining the upper hand.

NOTES

1. Fritiof Fryxell, "Grand Teton National Park," on reverse of U.S. Department of the Interior, Geological Survey, *Topographical Map of the Grand Teton National Park*; John C. Reed, Jr., "Geology of the Teton Range," in Leigh Ortenburger, *A Climber's Guide to the Teton Range*, 321–29.

2. Many of these items are on display in the Jackson Hole Museum, Jackson, Wyoming.

3. Elizabeth Wied Hayden, *From Trapper to Tourist in Jackson Hole*, 6.

4. Orrin H. and Lorraine G. Bonney, *Bonney's Guide*, 123.

5. Mosquito Creek Pass and Phillips Canyon Pass are also in this area and may have been used alternately with the Teton Pass route.

6. Philip A. Rollins (ed.), *The Discovery of the Oregon Trail*, Appendix B, 356–67, 348, 332–36.

7. *Ibid.*, 336.

8. *Ibid.*, 357–58.

9. A curious structure of standing rock slabs arranged in a circle, found on the summit of the high west spur of the Grand Teton, may

have been constructed by the Sheep Eaters. The structure is known to modern-day mountain climbers as The Enclosure.

Chapter 2

1. Stallo Vinton, *John Colter*, 27, 31.

2. Thomas James, *Three Years Among the Indians and Mexicans*, 58.

3. Reuben G. Thwaites (ed.), *Original Journals of the Lewis and Clark Expedition*, V, 242–43, 335.

4. *Ibid.*, 341–42.

5. Vinton, *op. cit.*, 43.

6. Hiram M. Chittenden, *The American Fur Trade of the Far West*, I, 114.

7. Paul C. Phillips, *The Fur Trade*, II, 260.

8. Vinton, op. cit., 45.

9. Nicholas Biddle, *History of the Expedition under the Command of Captains Lewis and Clark*, I and II.

10. J. Neilson Barry, "John Colter's Map of 1814," *Wyoming Annals*, X (July, 1938), 106.

11. William H. Goetzmann, *Exploration and Empire*, 24.

12. Chittenden, *Fur Trade*, II, 714–17, traces Colter along the following route: Fort Raymond, Pryor's Fork, Bighorn, Stinking Water, Wind River, Togwotee or Union Pass, Jackson Hole, Teton Pass, Pierre's Hole, Jackson Lake, Yellowstone Lake, Yellowstone River and Falls, cross country to Fort Raymond.

Phillips, *op. cit.*, II, 261, follows Colter from Fort Raymond to Pryor's Fork, Clark's Fork, Shoshone River, Wind River, Yellowstone Lake, and back to Fort Raymond.

Vinton, *op. cit.*, 57–62, traces the route from Fort Raymond to Pryor's Fork, Clark's Fork, Stinking Water River, Wind River, Union Pass, Gros Ventre River, Jackson Lake, Teton Pass, Pierre's Hole, Conant Pass, Yellowstone Lake, Yellowstone River, Clark's Fork, back to the Stinking Water, Bighorn River, Pryor's Fork, and Fort Raymond.

Burton Harris, *John Colter*, 98–114, describes the route as leading from Fort Raymond to Pryor's Fork, Clark's Fork, Shoshone River, Wind River, Togwotee Pass, Jackson Hole, Teton Pass, Pierre's Hole, Teton Pass, Jackson Lake, Yellowstone Lake, Yellowstone River, Clark's Fork, back to the Shoshone, Bighorn River, Pryor's Fork, and Fort Raymond.

Barry, "John Colter's Map," *loc. cit.*, 108–109, sees the sequence of locations as follows: Fort Raymond, Pryor's Fork, Sage Creek,

North Fork of the Shoshone River, Elk River, Ishawooa Pass, Pass Creek, Thorofare Creek, Atlantic Creek, Two Ocean Pass, Pacific Creek, Southwest Arm of Yellowstone Lake, West Thumb of Yellowstone Lake, back to North Fork of the Shoshone, Sage Creek, Pryor's Gap, Pryor's Fork, Fort Raymond.

13. See Washington Irving, *The Adventures of Captain Bonneville*, 252.

14. Merrill J. Mattes, "Behind the Legend of Colter's Hell: The Early Exploration of Yellowstone National Park," *Mississippi Valley Historical Review*, XXXVI (September, 1949), 257. W. T. Hamilton visited these same hot springs when they were dying out. See W. T. Hamilton, *My Sixty Years on the Plains*, 40.

15. Chittenden, *Fur Trade*, II, 715, n. 2. Vinton, *op. cit.*, 66, traces this quotation to an article by Brackenridge in the *Louisiana Gazette*, April 18, 1811.

16. Isabelle F. Story to Grace Raymond Hebard, September 19, 1934, p. 2, in the Grace Raymond Hebard Manuscript Collection, University of Wyoming Archives, Laramie.

17. In 1872, a government survey party passed through Pierre's Hole. It might be argued that one member of the group, John Merle Coulter, carved the stone. Misspelling of his own name can be forgiven, but the date on the other side hardly resembles 1872.

18. Chittenden, *Fur Trade*, II, 715.

19. James, *op. cit.*, 52–53.

20. Vinton, *op. cit.*, 61. But see note 17 above. It is arguable that "JC" was carved by John Merle Coulter, for whom the stream was named.

21. *Ibid.*, 61–62.

22. Harris, *op. cit.*, 111.

23. Chittenden, *Fur Trade*, I, 119.

24. James, *op. cit.*, 52–53.

25. Chittenden, *Fur Trade*, II, 717.

26. John Bradbury, *Travels in the Interior of America*, 44–47, n. 18 (by Bradbury).

27. *Ibid.*, 46, n. 18.

28. James, *op. cit.*, 57.

29. See indexed references to Colter in Thwaites, *Original Journals*.

30. Chittenden, *Fur Trade*, I, 137–38.

31. *Ibid.*, 140–41.

32. Elizabeth Hayden, *op. cit.*, 9.

33. Vinton, *op. cit.*, 97–99.

34. Chittenden, *Fur Trade*, I, 141.

35. Vinton, *op. cit.*, 102, 110.

Chapter 3

1. Rollins, *op. cit.*, *cv*.

2. Elizabeth Hayden, *op. cit.*, 9.

3. Rollins, *op. cit.*, Appendix A, 289. This section of Appendix A, entitled "Journey of Mr. Hunt and His Companions from Saint Louis to the Mouth of the Columbia by a New Route Across the Rocky Mountains," is a retranslation into English of the original translation of Wilson Price Hunt's diary into French in *Nouvelles Annales des Voyages* (Paris, 1821), X.

4. Chittenden, *Fur Trade*, I, 144–45.

5. Inferred from a passage in Rollins, *op. cit.*, Appendix A, 288.

6. Bradbury, *op. cit.*, 98.

7. Washington Irving, *Astoria*, 65.

8. *Ibid.*, 73.

9. Bradbury, *op. cit.*, 100.

10. Merrill J. Mattes, *Jackson Hole: Crossroads of the Western Fur Trade*, 1807–1840.

11. Rollins, *op. cit.*, Appendix A, 286.

12. *Ibid.*, 286–88.

13. Irving, *Astoria*, 371.

14. Rollins, *op. cit.*, Appendix A, 288.

15. *Ibid.*, 289–93.

16. Irving, *Astoria*, 490–91.

17. Rollins, *op. cit.*, 86, 111–13.

18. Irving, *Astoria*, 595–96, 665–69.

19. Rollins, *op. cit.*, 138.

20. *Ibid.*, 153–55.

21. *Ibid.*, 157–58. The italics are Stuart's.

22. *Ibid.*, 255.

23. Irving, *Astoria*, 585–86.

24. Gabriel Franchère, *Narrative of a Voyage to the Northwest Coast of America*, 296–301.

25. Irving, *Astoria*, 669.

26. Alexander Ross, *The Fur Hunters of the Far West*, I, 184.

27. *Ibid.*, 283.

28. Iroquois Indians had been coming west with the Canadian fur companies for years.

29. Ross, *Fur Hunters*, I, 200–201.

30. The number of men, six, is inferred from a passage in *ibid.*, 199.

31. Ross, *Fur Hunters*, I, 201.

32. Dale Morgan, *Jedediah Smith and the Opening of the West*, 127.

33. P. W. Norris, "Fifth Annual Report of the Superintendent of

the Yellowstone National Park," *House Executive Document No. 1,*
47th Cong., 1st sess., Part 5, 784–85.

34. Ross, *Fur Hunters,* I, 212, 276.

35. Phillips, *op. cit.,* II, 344–45.

36. Morgan, *op. cit.,* 120–25.

Chapter 4

1. Chittenden, *Fur Trade,* I, 262.

2. *Ibid.,* II, 958; I, 264–70.

3. Charles L. Camp (ed.), *James Clyman,* 22.

4. An excellent fictional account of Glass's crawl appears in Frederick Manfred's *Lord Grizzly.*

5. Daniel T. Potts to Robert T. Potts, July 16, 1826, published in the *Philadelphia Gazette and Daily Advertiser,* November 14, 1826, and reprinted in Donald M. Frost, "Notes on General Ashley, the Overland Trail, and South Pass," *Proceedings of the American Antiquarian Society,* LIV (October, 1944), 219.

6. Camp, *op. cit.,* 22.

7. Frost, "Notes," *loc. cit.,* 196.

8. Harrison Clifford Dale, *The Ashley-Smith Explorations,* 63.

9. The group is referred to as the Potts party because there is no record of its leader. Daniel T. Potts, however, was a subordinate who is definitely known to have been with the group.

10. Camp, *op. cit.,* 29.

11. It is a matter of dispute whether Stuart in fact crossed the Continental Divide at this point. Rollins, *op. cit.,* 255, maintains that he did. Dale, *op. cit.,* and Morgan, *op. cit.,* credit Jedediah Smith with the discovery of South Pass.

12. Irving, *Astoria,* 671.

13. Goetzmann, *Exploration and Empire,* map (N.B. addendum), 114.

14. Morgan, *op. cit.,* 128.

15. Frost, "Notes," *loc. cit.,* 207; Mattes, *Jackson Hole,* 101–102; Dale, *op. cit.,* 92.

16. *Missouri Advocate* and *St. Louis Enquirer,* October 29, 1825, in Frost, "Notes," *loc. cit.,* 300.

17. Morgan, *op. cit.,* 176.

18. *Ibid.,* 190; Mattes, *Jackson Hole,* 103.

19. Good accounts of trapping techniques appear in Irving, *Adventures of Captain Bonneville,* 471, and Frances Fuller Victor, *The River of the West,* 64.

20. Morgan, *op. cit.,* 187–89, 194.

21. Daniel T. Potts to Robert T. Potts, July 8, 1827, published

in the *Philadelphia Gazette and Daily Advertiser*, September 27, 1827, and reprinted in Frost, "Notes," *loc. cit.*, 219–20.

22. Frost, "Notes," *loc. cit.*, 209.

23. John E. Sunder, *Bill Sublette*, 70–76.

24. Victor, *op. cit.*, 58.

25. Merlin K. Potts, "The Mountain Men in Jackson Hole," in *Campfire Tales of Jackson Hole*, 18.

26. Victor, *op. cit.*, 84. The valley might have been called Davey's Hole, as well as Jackson's Hole, by some of Jackson's closest friends.

27. Washington Irving, *The Rocky Mountains*, 1st ed. (1837). This is the original title of Irving's *Adventures of Captain Bonneville*.

28. Victor, *op. cit.*, 58, 75–76, 84–85.

29. Morgan, *op. cit.*, 316–30; Sunder, *op. cit.*, 122, n. 15.

Chapter 5

1. Benjamin Waterhouse and John B. Wyeth, *Oregon*, 60–61.

2. Nathaniel J. Wyeth, "Journal of 1832," in Archer B. Hulbert (ed.), *The Call of the Columbia*, 120.

3. Waterhouse and Wyeth, *Oregon*, 72.

4. Warren A. Ferris, *Life in the Rocky Mountains*, 156.

5. *Ibid.*, 159. Irving claims that another party under Captain Benjamin Bonneville buried the bones of Moore and Foy. See Irving, *Adventures of Captain Bonneville*, 122.

6. Chittenden, *Fur Trade*, I, 299.

7. Ferris, *op. cit.*, 204–205.

8. *Ibid.*, 212, n. 12 (by Ferris).

9. Chittenden, *Fur Trade*, I, 364.

10. Archer B. and Dorothy P. Hulbert (eds.), *The Oregon Crusade*, 205.

11. Samuel Parker, *Journal of an Exploring Tour Beyond the Rocky Mountains*, 87.

12. *Ibid.*, 90–91.

13. *Ibid.* The italics are Parker's.

14. *Ibid.*, 92.

15. *Ibid.*, 359–93.

16. Osborne Russell, *Journal of a Trapper*, 42–43.

17. *Ibid.*, 43–47.

18. Victor, *op. cit.*, 233. See also James B. Marsh, *Four Years in the Rockies*, 181–82.

19. Russell, *op. cit.*, 62.

20. *Ibid.*, 91.

21. Robert Newell, "Journal," quoted in Mattes, *Jackson Hole*, 28.

22. Russell, *op. cit.*, 102–103, 107.

23. Hiram M. Chittenden and Alfred T. Richardson (eds.), *Life, Letters and Travels of Father Pierre-Jean De Smet, S.J., 1801–1873,* I, 222.

Chapter 6

1. It was probably designated South Pass in order to distinguish it from the northern pass discovered by Lewis and Clark.

2. Chittenden, *Fur Trade,* II, 715, n. 2.

3. Dale, *op. cit.,* 92–93, n. 169. Dale found this document in the Washington Hood Manuscript Collection, Missouri Historical Society, St. Louis.

4. David Lavender, *American Heritage History of the Great West,* 177–279.

5. Goetzmann, *Exploration and Empire,* 231–64.

6. *Ibid.,* 281–86.

7. *Ibid.*

8. Captain Andrew A. Humphreys to Captain William F. Raynolds, April 13, 1859, as reprinted in William F. Raynolds, "Report," *Senate Executive Document No. 77,* 40th Cong., 2d [erroneously printed "1st"] sess., 4.

9. Raynolds, "Report," *loc. cit.,* 86.

10. *Ibid.,* 88–93.

11. *Ibid.,* 93.

12. *Ibid.,* 93–96.

13. *Ibid.,* 14.

Chapter 7

1. Walter W. De Lacy, "A Trip up the South Snake River in 1863," *Contributions to the Historical Society of Montana,* I (1876), 113–18.

2. Lavender, *Great West,* 308, 319–20.

3. In both Elizabeth Hayden, *op. cit.,* 23, and Bonney and Bonney, *op. cit.,* 107, the De Lacy campsite is mistakenly located on Buffalo River instead of Pacific Creek. A careful reading of pp. 124–25 in De Lacy's "A Trip up the South Snake River in 1863" reveals, however, that the miners only *paused* at the mouth of the Buffalo, then moved up the Snake a few miles to Pacific Creek, where they camped. An excerpt from De Lacy should clear up the controversy: ". . . we came to another large valley, through which ran a stream coming from the east . . . . The Country about us was an open prairie, and the stream was no doubt what Dr. Hayden [a later surveyor] calls the Buffalo fork of Snake River. I halted the men at the creek as they came up, and when all had arrived I suggested to them that we

should *go on to the next water* [italics added], pick out a good camp, and remain some days and prospect the different streams which were in sight. This was agreed to, and we went forward about three [closer to two] miles to the next creek [Pacific Creek], near the outlet of Lake Jackson . . . and established ourselves where wood, water, and grass were abundant."

4. De Lacy, "Trip," *loc. cit.*, 125–26.

5. *Ibid.*, 127.

6. Norris, "Fifth Annual Report," *loc. cit.*, 788.

Chapter 8

1. Gustavus C. Doane, "Report on the Yellowstone Expedition of 1870," *Senate Executive Document No. 51*, 41st Cong., 3d sess.; William T. Jackson, "The Washburn-Doane Expedition into the Upper Yellowstone, 1870," *Pacific Historical Review*, X (June, 1941), 189–208.

2. J. W. Barlow, "Report of a Reconnaissance in Wyoming and Montana Territories, 1871," *Senate Executive Document No. 66*, 42d Cong., 2d sess.

3. Ferdinand V. Hayden, *Preliminary Report of the United States Geological Survey of Montana and Portions of Adjacent Territories, Being a Fifth Annual Report.*

4. Ferdinand V. Hayden, *Sixth Annual Report*, 1–10.

5. Goetzmann, *Exploration and Empire*, 512–13.

6. Nathaniel P. Langford, "The Ascent of Mount Hayden," *Scribner's Monthly*, IV (June, 1873), 129–37.

7. William H. Jackson, *Time Exposure*, 208. A seventeen-year-old Englishman who was one of the other three to begin the ascent with Stevenson and Langford did not doubt that the latter two "got to the top." See "Exploring the Yellowstone with Hayden, 1872: Diary of Sidford Hamp," ed. by Herbert O. Brayer, *Annals of Wyoming*, XIV (1942), 274–76.

8. Ortenburger, *op. cit.*, 105–108.

9. Goetzmann, *Exploration and Empire*, 500.

10. William H. Jackson and Howard R. Driggs, *The Pioneer Photographer*, 126.

11. Frank H. Bradley, "Report," in Ferdinand Hayden, *Sixth Annual Report*, 269.

12. *Ibid.*, 263–65, and map between pp. 244 and 245.

13. Ferdinand V. Hayden, "Preliminary Report . . . for the Season of 1877," *House Executive Document No. 1*, 45th Cong., 2d sess., Part 5, 763–78; Orestes St. John, "Report of Orestes St. John,

Geologist of the Teton Division," in Ferdinand V. Hayden, *Eleventh Annual Report*, 321–508.

14. Orestes St. John, "Report on the Geology of the Wind River District," in Ferdinand V. Hayden, *Twelfth Annual Report*, I, 173–270.

15. Jackson and Driggs, *op. cit.*, 296.

16. W. H. Holmes, "Report," in Hayden, *Twelfth Annual Report*, II, 2–3. Two of these plates are printed in *ibid.*, I, following p. 270.

17. William A. Jones, "Report," *House Executive Document No. 285*, 43d Cong., 1st sess.

18. Merlin K. Potts, "The Doane Expedition of 1876–77," in *Campfire Tales of Jackson Hole*, 20–37. Potts consulted a copy of Doane's original manuscript on file in the park headquarters library, Grand Teton National Park, Moose, Wyoming.

19. I am indebted to William H. Goetzmann's *Exploration and Empire* for much of my evaluation of Hayden's surveys.

Chapter 9

1. John W. Hoyt, "Report," *House Executive Document No. 1*, 47th Cong., 1st sess., Part 5, 1074–77.

2. Philip H. Sheridan, *Report of an Exploration of Parts of Wyoming, Idaho, and Montana, in August and September, 1882*.

3. Now known as Sheridan Pass.

4. D. B. Sacket, "Report of the Inspector General," *House Executive Document No. 1*, 47th Cong., 2d sess., Part 2, 76.

5. Freeman Tilden, *Following the Frontier with F. Jay Haynes*, 115–39.

6. Arnold Hague, "Report," *House Executive Document No. 1*, 49th Cong., 2d sess., Part 5, 54–59.

7. Barton W. Evermann, "A Reconnaissance of the Streams and Lakes of Western Montana and Northwestern Wyoming," *Bulletin of the United States Fish Commission*, XI (1891).

8. William G. D. Stewart, *Altowan*.

9. William A. Baillie-Grohman, *Fifteen Years' Sport and Life in the Hunting Grounds of Western America and British Columbia*.

10. William A. Baillie-Grohman, *Camps in the Rockies*.

11. Tilden, *op. cit.*, 223–45.

12. Richard Leigh, "Writings of Richard 'Beaver Dick' Leigh of Jackson Hole, Wyoming," ed. by Flora Edeen, on file in the Richard Leigh Manuscript Collection, University of Wyoming Archives.

Chapter 10

1. Information about the early settlers of Jackson Hole is found

mainly in Bonney and Bonney, *op. cit.*; Elizabeth Hayden, *op. cit.*; Nolie Mumey, *The Teton Mountains*; and Roland W. Brown, Jr. (ed.), *Souvenir History of Jackson Hole*. Unless otherwise identified in footnotes, all subsequent references to them are based on accounts in these four sources.

2. Frances Judge, "Mountain River Men," in *Campfire Tales of Jackson Hole*, 52–58.

3. Mumey, *op. cit.*, 359–61.

4. For further information on the Togwotee Pass road, see J. C. Sanford, "Report," *House Miscellaneous Document No. 245*, 55th Cong., 3d sess.

Chapter 11

1. Fritiof Fryxell, "Prospector of Jackson Hole," in *Campfire Tales of Jackson Hole*, 47–51.

2. Struthers Burt, *The Diary of a Dude Wrangler*, 290–91; *Wyoming State Journal*, September 8, 1927, on file in the Jackson Hole Manuscript Collection, University of Wyoming Archives; see also an untitled manuscript containing quotations from Lee L. Lucas, an early settler, in the same collection.

3. The unnamed newspaper is quoted extensively in Bonney and Bonney, *op. cit.*, 118–20.

4. Owen Wister, *Owen Wister Out West*, 52–58.

5. Owen Wister, *The Virginian*, 304–305.

6. Bonney and Bonney, *op. cit.*, 53.

7. *New York Times*, July 31, 1914, p. 8.

8. Roald Fryxell, "The Affair at Cunningham's Cabin," in *Campfire Tales of Jackson Hole*, 43–46.

9. Fritiof Fryxell, "The Story of Deadman's Bar," in *Campfire Tales of Jackson Hole*, 38–42.

10. *New York Times*, July 27, 1895, p. 1.

11. "In re Race Horse," *Federal Reporter*, LXX, 598–613.

12. "John H. Ward v. Race Horse," *United States Supreme Court Reports*, CLXIII, 244–50.

13. D. M. Browning, "Report of the Commissioner of Indian Affairs," *House Miscellaneous Document No. 5*, 54th Cong., 1st sess., 60–80; D. M. Browning, "Report of the Commissioner of Indian Affairs," *House Miscellaneous Document No. 5*, 54th Cong., 2d sess., 56–70.

14. Bonney and Bonney, *op. cit.*, 43, 112.

15. *Ibid.*, 47, 49, 95, 133–34.

Chapter 12

1. *Jackson's Hole Courier*, May 13, 1920, in Jackson Hole Manuscript Collection; Associated Press, "Town Set Good Pace," Jackson Hole Manuscript Collection.

2. "New Rule of Queens," Jackson Hole Manuscript Collection.

Chapter 13

1. Elizabeth Hayden, *op. cit.*, 40.
2. Mumey, *op. cit.*, 286, 299–300.
3. Bonney and Bonney, *op. cit.*, 49.
4. Wister, *Owen Wister Out West*.
5. Elizabeth Hayden, *op. cit.*, 41.
6. Burt, *Diary of a Dude Wrangler*, 120.
7. *Jackson Hole Guide*, December 15, 1966.
8. Bonney and Bonney, *op. cit.*, 90, 128; Brown, *op. cit.*, 25–26.

Chapter 14

1. Elizabeth Hayden, *op. cit.*, 39; see also Elliott H. Paul, *Desperate Scenery*.

2. Margaret E. and Olaus J. Murie, *Wapiti Wilderness*, 117–18.

3. *Ibid.*; Frank C. Emerson, *Seventeenth Biennial Report of the State Engineer*, 23–24; Jenny and Leigh Lakes Irrigation Papers, Files of the National Park Service, Grand Teton National Park, File 606, National Archives, Washington, D.C.

4. Burt, *Diary of a Dude Wrangler*, 120.

5. T. S. Brandegee, "Teton Forest Reserve," *House Document No. 5*, 55th Cong., 3d sess., 191–206.

6. S. B. M. Young, "Supplemental Report," *House Miscellaneous Document No. 5*, 55th Cong., 2d sess., 794–806.

7. Thomas Ryan, "Letter from the Secretary of the Interior . . . Relative to the Region in Question," *Senate Document No. 39*, 55th Cong., 3d sess.

8. Thomas Ryan, "Letter from the Secretary of the Interior . . . Yellowstone National Park," *House Miscellaneous Document No. 500*, 57th Cong., 1st sess.

9. *Ibid.*

10. Leo H. Diederich *et al.* (eds.), *Jackson Hole National Monument, Wyoming*, I, 1.

11. Chester C. Anderson, *The Elk of Jackson Hole*, 24.

12. *Ibid.*; Dillon Wallace, "Saddle and Camp in the Rockies: The Tragedy of the Elk," *Outing*, LVIII (May, 1911), 187–201, and "Saddle and Camp in the Rockies: The End of the Trail," *Outing*, LVIII (June, 1911), 319–33.

Chapter 15

1. John Ise, *Our National Park Policy*, 324–25.

2. Horace M. Albright to Wilford W. Neilson, April 5, 1933, reprinted in Vanderbilt Webb (ed.), *Mr. John D. Rockefeller, Jr.'s Proposed Gift*, 1 ff. Albright's role in the history of Jackson Hole was retold to me in an interview in New York on October 18, 1967.

3. H. R. 11661, 65th Cong., 2d sess.

4. H. R. 13350, 65th Cong., 3d sess.

5. *Congressional Record*, 65th Cong., 3d sess., 4567; Diederich *et al., op. cit.*, Vol. II, Part 2, Exhibit 4.

6. H. R. 1412, 66th Cong., 1st sess.

7. Albright to Neilson, *loc. cit.*; U.S. Congress, Senate, *Hearings . . . Pursuant to S. Res. 226 (72d Congress)*, 73d Cong., 2d sess., 152.

8. Albright to Neilson, *loc. cit.*

9. *Ibid.*

10. See National Park Service annual report for 1918.

11. Albright to Neilson, *loc. cit.*

12. *Ibid.*; Jenny and Leigh Lakes Irrigation Papers, Files of the National Park Service, Yellowstone National Park, File 584, and Grand Teton National Park, File 606, National Archives.

13. Henry G. Watson, "Power Possibilities in Wyoming," in *Fifteenth Biennial Report of the State Engineer*, 66.

14. Frank C. Emerson, *Seventeenth Biennial Report*, frontispiece, 23–24.

15. See National Park Service annual reports for 1920 through 1925.

16. Albright to Neilson, *loc. cit.*; *Hearings . . . Pursuant to S. Res. 226*, 155–58.

17. *Ibid.*

18. *Ibid.*; U.S. Congress, Senate, *Hearing . . . Pursuant to S. Res. 237*, 69th Cong., 1st sess.; Verne E. Chatelain, "A Memorandum Dealing with the Question of the Jackson Hole Region," 21–22, Files of the National Park Service, Grand Teton National Park, File 602–01, National Archives.

19. *Hearings . . . Pursuant to S. Res. 226*, 267.

20. S. 3427, 69th Cong., 1st sess.

21. *Hearing . . . Pursuant to S. Res. 237*; Chatelain, "Memorandum," 24–25.

Chapter 16

1. Albright to Neilson, *loc. cit.*; *Hearings . . . Pursuant to S. Res. 226*, 158.

2. Harold P. Fabian to Wilford W. Neilson, April 6, 1933, reprinted in Webb, *op. cit.*, 42 ff.; *Hearings . . . Pursuant to S. Res. 226.*

3. Correspondence in Files of the National Park Service, Grand Teton National Park, File 606, National Archives.

4. Vanderbilt Webb to Robert Miller, February 21, 1928, reprinted in *Hearings . . . Pursuant to S. Res. 226*, 40.

5. Harold Fabian to Robert Miller, May 3, 1928, quoted in *Hearings . . . Pursuant to S. Res. 226*, 40.

6. U.S. Congress, Senate, *Hearings before the Committee . . . Pursuant to S. Res.* 237, 70th Cong., 2d sess.

7. U.S. Congress, Senate, *Hearings . . . Pursuant to S. Res. 250* (*75th Congress*), 75th Cong., 3d sess., 242.

8. Albright interview, October 18, 1967. See also Horace M. Albright to John D. Rockefeller, Jr., February 16, 1927, reprinted in U.S. Congress, House, *Hearings . . . on H. R. 2241*, 78th Cong., 1st sess., 164.

9. *S. 5543*, 70th Cong., 2d sess.

10. Albright to Neilson, *loc. cit.*; Chatelain, "Memorandum," 81.

Chapter 17

1. Harold Fabian to Vanderbilt Webb, August 28, 1929, and Harold Fabian to Vanderbilt Webb, September 4, 1929, in Chatelain, "Memorandum," 55–62.

2. Commission on the Conservation of the Jackson Hole Elk, *The Conservation of the Elk of Jackson Hole, Wyoming.*

3. Commission on the Conservation of the Jackson Hole Elk, *Proceedings of the Second Meeting.*

4. Chatelain, "Memorandum," 41.

5. Fabian to Webb, August 28, 1929, *loc. cit.*, 58–62.

6. Correspondence in Files of the National Park Service, Grand Teton National Park, File 602–01, Part 1, File 606, National Archives.

7. Chatelain, "Memorandum," 67–68.

8. Fabian to Webb, August 28, 1929, *loc. cit.*, 61–62.

9. Murie and Murie, *op. cit.*, 121.

10. Files of the National Park Service, Grand Teton National Park, File 602–01, Part 1.

11. Chatelain, "Memorandum," 87.

12. *Hearings . . . on H. R. 2241*, 381.

13. Frederic Irland, "The Wyoming Game Stronghold," *Scribner's Magazine*, XXXIV (September, 1903), 275.

14. Ise, *op. cit.*, 493.

15. Fabian to Neilson, April 6, 1933, *loc. cit.*

16. *Hearings . . . Pursuant to S. Res. 226.*

17. Albert W. Gabbey Papers, Files of the National Park Service, Grand Teton National Park, File 610, National Archives.

18. S. 3705, 73rd Cong., 2nd sess.

19. Diederich *et al.*, *op. cit.*, Vol. II, Part 2, Exhibit 9.

20. S. 2972, 74th Cong., 1st sess.

21. Diederich *et al.*, *op. cit.*, Vol. II, Part 2, Exhibit 11.

22. *Hearings . . . Pursuant to S. Res. 250.*

23. *Ibid.*; *Hearings . . . on H. R. 2241.*

Chapter 18

1. John D. Rockefeller, Jr., to Harold L. Ickes, November 27, 1942, reprinted in Diederich *et al.*, *op. cit.*, Vol. II, Part 2, Exhibit 13.

2. *Ibid.*, Exhibits 12, 14, 15.

3. *Ibid.*, Exhibit 17.

4. "State of Wyoming v. Franke," *Federal Supplement*, LVIII, 96. See also Diederich *et al.*, *op. cit.*, Vol. II, Part 3, Exhibits 34, 42.

5. H. R. 2241, 78th Cong., 1st sess.

6. Diederich *et al.*, *op. cit.*, Vol. II, Part 3, Exhibit 39.

7. H. R. 5469, 78th Cong., 2d sess.; H. R. 1292, 79th Cong., 1st sess.

8. Diederich *et al.*, *op. cit.*, Vol. II, Part 2, Exhibits 16, 35–40.

9. *Ibid.*, Exhibit 30.

10. *Ibid.*, Exhibit 32.

11. S. 3409, 81st Cong., 1st sess.

12. Diederich *et al.*, *op. cit.*, Vol. II, Part 4, Exhibit 63.

13. *Ibid.*

Chapter 19

1. Gordon Graham, *A Study of the Economy of Jackson, Wyoming: November 1, 1966*, 12.

2. Elizabeth Hayden, *op. cit.*, 41–44.

3. James Lipscomb, "72 Hours of Terror," *Sports Illustrated*, XXII (June 14, 1965), 86–104, and "Night of the One-eyed Devils," *Sports Illustrated*, XXII (June 21, 1965), 64–77.

4. See *Jackson Hole Guide*, September 28, 1967, editorial.

5. *Jackson Hole Guide*, December 1, 1966; and Bonney and Bonney, *op. cit.*, 58–59, 110, 125.

BIBLIOGRAPHY

Primary Sources

GOVERNMENT DOCUMENTS

(Published by the U.S. Government Printing Office, Washington, D.C., unless otherwise noted.)

Antweiler, J. C., and J. D. Love. *Gold-bearing Sedimentary Rocks in Northwest Wyoming—A Preliminary Report*. U.S. Department of the Interior, Geological Survey *Circular 541*. Washington, 1967.

Barlow, J. W. "Report of a Reconnaissance in Wyoming and Montana Territories, 1871," *Senate Executive Document No. 66*, 42d Cong., 2d sess. Serial No. 1479. Washington, 1872.

Brandegee, T. S. "Teton Forest Reserve," *House Docu-*

ment No. 5, 55th Cong., 3d sess. Serial No. 3763. Washington, 1899.

Browning, D. M. "Report of the Commissioner of Indian Affairs," *House Miscellaneous Document No. 5*, 54th Cong., 1st sess. Serial No. 3382. Washington, 1896.

———. "Report of the Commissioner of Indian Affairs," *House Miscellaneous Document No. 5*, 54th Cong., 2d sess. Serial No. 3489. Washington, 1897.

Chatelain, Verne E. "A Memorandum Dealing with the Question of the Jackson Hole Region in Wyoming in its Relation to the National Park Service." ca. 1932. Unpublished paper in the Files of the National Park Service, Grand Teton National Park, File 602–01, National Archives, Washington, D.C.

Commission on the Conservation of the Jackson Hole Elk. *The Conservation of the Elk of Jackson Hole, Wyoming: A Report to Hon. Dwight F. Davis, the Secretary of War, Chairman of the President's Committee on Outdoor Recreation, and Hon. Frank C. Emerson, Governor of Wyoming.* Washington, 1927.

———. *Proceedings of the Second Meeting of the Commission on the Conservation of the Elk of Jackson Hole, Wyoming, Held at Washington, D.C., December 4–5, 1929.* Washington, ca. 1930.

Diederich, Leo H., *et al.* (eds.) *Jackson Hole National Monument, Wyoming: A Compendium of Important Papers Covering Negotiation in the Establishment and Administration of the National Monument.* 4 vols. Washington, ca. 1945, 1950. (Vol. I, chronology and index; Vol. II, unpublished papers; Vol. III, printed hearings and documents [see entries elsewhere in this bibliography under U.S. Congress]; Vol. IV, maps.)

Doane, Gustavus C. "Report on the Yellowstone Expedition of 1870," *Senate Executive Document No. 51,* 41st Cong., 3d sess. Serial No. 1440. Washington, 1871.

Emerson, Frank C. *Seventeenth Biennial Report of the State Engineer to the Governor of Wyoming, 1923–1924.* Cheyenne, 1924.

Evermann, Barton W. "A Reconnaissance of the Streams and Lakes of Western Montana and Northwestern Wyoming," *Bulletin of the United States Fish Commission,* XI (1891). (Reprinted in *House Miscellaneous Documents No. 112,* 52d Cong., 2d sess. Serial No. 3129. Washington, 1893.)

Gannett, Henry "Geographic Fieldwork of the Yellowstone Park Division." In Ferdinand V. Hayden, *Twelfth Annual Report of the United States Geological and Geographical Survey of the Territories,* II. Washington, 1883.

Hague, Arnold. "Report," *House Executive Document No. 1,* 49th Cong., 1st sess., Part 5. Serial No. 2380. Washington, 1886.

Hayden, Ferdinand V. *Eleventh Annual Report of the United States Geological and Geographical Survey of the Territories Embracing Idaho and Wyoming, Being a Report of Progress of the Exploration for the Year 1877.* Washington, 1879.

———. "Preliminary Report of the Field-work of the United States Geological and Geographical Survey of the Territories, under the Direction of Prof. F. V. Hayden, for the Season of 1877," *House Executive Document No. 1,* 45th Cong., 2d sess., Part 5. Serial No. 1800. Washington, 1877.

———. *Preliminary Report of the United States Geological Survey of Montana and Portions of Adjacent Territories, Being a Fifth Annual Report of Progress.* 1872.

(Also printed in *House Executive Document No. 326*, 42d Cong., 2d sess. Serial No. 1520. Washington, 1872.

———. *Sixth Annual Report of the United States Geological Survey of the Territories, Embracing Portions of Montana, Idaho, Wyoming, and Utah, Being a Report of Progress of the Exploration for the Year 1872.* Washington, 1873. (Also printed in *House Miscellaneous Document No. 112*, 42d Cong., 3d sess. Serial No. 1573. Washington, 1873.)

———. *Twelfth Annual Report of the United States Geological and Geographical Survey of the Territories: A Report of Progress of the Exploration in Wyoming and Idaho for the Year 1878.* 2 vols. and atlas. Washington, 1883.

Hoyt, John W. "Report of the Governor of the Territory of Wyoming," *House Executive Document No. 1*, 47th Cong., 1st sess., Part 5. Serial No. 2018. Washington, 1881.

Jones, William A. "Report upon the Reconnaissance of Northwestern Wyoming, made in the Summer of 1873," *House Executive Document No. 285*, 43d Cong., 1st sess. Serial No. 1615. Washington, 1874.

Norris, P. W. "Fifth Annual Report of the Superintendent of the Yellowstone National Park," *House Executive Document No. 1*, 47th Cong., 1st sess., Part 5. Serial No. 2018. Washington, 1881.

Preble, Edward A. *Report on Condition of Elk in Jackson Hole, Wyoming, in 1911.* U.S. Department of Agriculture, Biological Survey *Bulletin 40.* Washington, 1911.

Raynolds, William F. "Report . . . on the Exploration of the Yellowstone and Missouri Rivers, in 1859–'60," *Senate Executive Document No. 77*, 40th Cong., 2d (erroneously printed "1st") sess. Serial No. 1317. Washington, 1868.

Ryan, Thomas. "Letter from the Secretary of the Interior, Transmitting with Accompanying Papers, the Draft of a Bill Providing for the Extension of the Limits of the Yellowstone National Park," *House Miscellaneous Document No. 500*, 57th Cong., 1st sess. Serial No. 4361. Washington, 1902.

———. "Letter from the Secretary of the Interior, Transmitting, in Response to Resolution of Senate of December 6, 1898, Copy of a Report from the Director of the Geological Survey, Giving Detailed Information Touching the Region South of and Adjoining the Yellowstone National Park, and also Excerpts from the Report of the Secretary of the Interior for the Fiscal Year Ended June 30, 1898, under the Head of the Yellowstone National Park, Relative to the Region in Question," *Senate Document No. 39*, 55th Cong., 3d sess. Serial No. 3728. Washington, 1899. (The director of the Geological Survey whose report is printed herein was Charles D. Walcott.)

Sacket, D. B. "Report of the Inspector General," *House Executive Document No. 1*, 47th Cong., 2d sess., Part 2. Serial No. 2091. Washington, 1882.

St. John, Orestes. "Report of Orestes St. John, Geologist of the Teton Division." In Ferdinand V. Hayden, *Eleventh Annual Report of the United States Geological and Geographical Survey of the Territories Embracing Idaho and Wyoming*, 321–508.

———. "Report on the Geology of the Wind River District." In Ferdinand V. Hayden, *Twelfth Annual Report of the United States Geological and Geographical Survey of the Territories*, I, 173–270.

Sanford, J. C. "Report." In "Letter from the Secretary of War, Transmitting, with a Letter from the Chief of Engineers, a Copy of a Report on the Construction of a Military Road from Fort Washakie, Wyo., to the Mouth of the Buffalo Fork of Snake River, Wyoming," *House Miscellaneous Document No. 245,* 55th Cong., 3d sess. Serial No. 3812. Washington, 1899. (Contains prints of photographs taken by a hunting party which had preceded Sanford's expedition into Jackson Hole.)

Sheridan, Philip H. *Report of an Exploration of Parts of Wyoming, Idaho, and Montana, in August and September, 1882, made by Lieut. Gen. P. H. Sheridan, Commanding the Military Division of the Missouri, with the Itinerary of Col. Jas. F. Gregory, and a Geological and Botanical Report by Surgeon W. H. Forwood.* Washington, 1882.

U.S. Congress. *Congressional Record.*

————, House. *Hearings Before the Committee on the Public Lands, . . . on H. R. 2241, a Bill to Abolish the Jackson Hole National Monument as Created by Presidential Proclamation Numbered 2578, Dated March 15, 1943, and to Restore the Area Embraced within and Constituting Said Monument to Its Status as Part of the Teton National Forest,* March 14, 26–28, June 1, 8–9, 1943, 78th Cong., 1st sess. Washington, 1943. (Included in Leo H. Diederich *et al.* [eds.], *Jackson Hole National Monument, Wyoming,* Vol. III, Exhibit 7.)

————. *Hearings Before the Subcommittee of the Committee on Public Lands, . . . on H. R. 1330, a Bill to Abolish the Jackson Hole National Monument as Created by Presidential Proclamation . . . , and to Restore the Lands Belonging to the United States*

Within the Exterior Boundaries of Said Monument to the Same Status Held Immediately Prior to the Issuance of Said Proclamation, April 14–18, 1947, 80th Cong., 1st sess. Washington, 1948. (Included in Leo H. Diederich *et al.* [eds.], *Jackson Hole National Monument, Wyoming,* Vol. III, Exhibit 9.)

U.S. Congress, Senate. *Hearing Before a Subcommittee of the Committee on Public Lands and Surveys, . . . Pursuant to S. Res. 237, . . . ,* August 18, 1926, 69th Cong., 1st sess. Washington, 1927. (Included in Leo H. Diederich *et al.* [eds.], *Jackson Hole National Monument, Wyoming,* Vol. III, Exhibit 3.)

———. *Hearings Before a Subcommittee of the Committee on Public Lands and Surveys, . . . Pursuant to S. Res. 237, a Resolution to Investigate the Advisability of Changing the Boundaries of Yellowstone National Park and Certain Other Parks,* July 19, 22–23, 1928, 70th Cong., 2d sess. Washington, 1928. (Included in Leo H. Diederich *et al.* [eds.], *Jackson Hole National Monument, Wyoming,* Vol. III, Exhibit 4.)

———. *Hearings Before a Subcommittee of the Committee on Public Lands and Surveys, . . . Pursuant to S. Res. 226 (72nd Congress), a Resolution to Investigate Activities in Connection with the Proposed Enlargement of the Yellowstone and Grand Teton National Parks,* August 7–10, 1933, 73d Cong., 2d sess. Washington, 1934. (Included in Leo H. Diederich *et al.* [eds.], *Jackson Hole National Monument, Wyoming,* Vol. III, Exhibit 5.)

———. *Hearings Before a Subcommittee on Public Lands and Surveys, . . . Pursuant to S. Res. 250 (75th Congress), a Resolution to Investigate the Questions of the Feasibility of Enlarging Grand Teton National Park in Wyoming,* August 8, 10, 1938, 75th Cong., 3d sess. Washington, 1939. (Included in Leo H. Diederich *et al.* [eds.], *Jackson Hole National Monument, Wyoming,* Vol. III, Exhibit 6.)

U.S. Department of the Interior, Geological Survey. *Heavy Metals Program Progress Report 1966 and 1967.* Geological Survey *Circular 560.* Washington, 1958. (Estimates that the Jackson Hole country contains more than fifty cubic miles of gold-bearing conglomerate, pp. 14–15.)

———, National Park Service. *Annual Reports of the Director.* Washington, 1918–67.

———. *A Report by the National Park Service on the Proposal to Extend the Boundaries of Grand Teton National Park, Wyoming, July, 1938.* Washington, 1938. (Included in Leo H. Diederich *et al.* [eds.], *Jackson Hole National Monument, Wyoming,* Vol. II, Part 1.

Watson, Henry G. "Power Possibilities in Wyoming." In *Fifteenth Biennial Report of the State Engineer to the Governor of Wyoming, 1919–1920.* Laramie, 1921.

Young, S. B. M. "Supplemental Report of the Acting Superintendent of Yellowstone Park," *House Miscellaneous Document No. 5,* 55th Cong., 2d sess., Serial No. 3642. Washington, 1897.

JUDICIAL DECISIONS

"In re Race Horse," *Federal Reporter,* LXX, 598–613. St. Paul, Minn., West Publishing Company, 1896.

"John H. Ward v. Race Horse," *United States Supreme Court Reports,* CLXIII, 505–20. In Lawyers Edition, Book XLI. Rochester, N.Y., Lawyers Co-operative, 1901.

"State of Wyoming v. Franke," *Federal Supplement,* LVIII, 890–97. St. Paul, Minn., West Publishing Company, 1945.

PUBLISHED CONTEMPORARY NARRATIVES, JOURNALS, DIARIES, AND LETTERS

Baillie-Grohman, William A. *Camps in the Rockies.* New York, Charles Scribner's Sons, 1882.

———. *Fifteen Years' Sport and Life in the Hunting Grounds of Western America and British Columbia.* London, H. Cox, 1900.

Biddle, Nicholas. *History of the Expedition under the Command of Captains Lewis and Clark.* Ed. by Paul Allen. 2 vols. Philadelphia, Bradford and Inskeep, 1814. (This work is a paraphrased version of the original Lewis and Clark journals and has been republished as James K. Hosmer [ed.], *History of the Expedition of Captains Lewis and Clark, 1804–5–6.* 2 vols. Chicago, A. C. McClurg and Company, 1902.)

Bonner, T. D. *The Life and Adventures of James P. Beckwourth, Mountaineer, Scout, and Pioneer, and Chief of the Crow Nation of Indians.* Ed. by Bernard DeVoto. New York, Alfred A. Knopf, 1931. (The original 1856 edition was supposedly based upon Beckwourth's dictation.)

Brackenridge, Henry M. *Journal of a Voyage up the River Missouri Performed in Eighteen Hundred and Eleven by H. M. Brackenridge, Esq.* Vol. VI in Reuben G. Thwaites (ed.), *Early Western Travels, 1748–1846.* (The first edition, entitled *Views of Louisiana,* published in Pittsburgh in 1814 by Cramer, Spear and Eichbaum. The second edition, with the new title, published in Baltimore in 1816 by Coale and Maxwell.)

Bradbury, John. *Travels in the Interior of North America in the Years 1809, 1810, and 1811.* Vol. V in Reuben G. Thwaites (ed.), *Early Western Travels, 1748–1846.* (First edition published in 1817. Second edition published in London in 1819 by Sherwood, Neely and Jones. Appendix III in the Thwaites edition contains Ramsay Crooks's narrative of Wilson Price Hunt's 1811–12 expedition.)

Burt, Struthers. *The Diary of a Dude Wrangler.* New York, Charles Scribner's Sons, 1925.

Camp, Charles L. (ed.). *James Clyman: American Frontiersman, 1792–1881.* San Francisco, California Historical Society, 1928. (Based on Clyman's diaries and reminiscences.)

Chittenden, Hiram M., and Alfred T. Richardson (eds.). *Life, Letters, and Travels of Father Pierre-Jean De Smet, S.J., 1801–1873.* 4 vols. New York, F. P. Harper, 1905.

Coues, Elliott (ed.). *New Light on the Early History of the Great Northwest: The Manuscript Journals of Alexander Henry, Fur Trader of the Northwest Company, and of David Thompson, Official Geographer and Explorer of the Same Company, 1799–1814.* 3 vols. New York, F. P. Harper, 1897.

Cox, Ross. *Adventures on the Columbia River, Including the Narrative of a Residence of Six Years on the Western Side of the Rocky Mountains, among Various Tribes of Indians Hitherto Unknown: Together with a Journey across the American Continent.* New York, J. & J. Harper, 1832. (Republished as *The Columbia River* in 1957 by the University of Oklahoma Press under the editorship of Edgar I. and Jane R. Stewart.

Cox sailed aboard the *Tonquin* to Fort Astoria with Astor's Pacific Fur Company. He later conducted a trans-Canadian expedition for the North West Company.)

Coyner, David H. *The Lost Trappers: A Collection of Interesting Scenes and Events in the Rocky Mountains; Together with a Short Description of California: Also, Some Account of the Fur Trade, Especially as Carried on About the Sources of the Missouri, Yellow Stone, and on the Waters of the Columbia in the Rocky Mountains.* Cincinnati, E. D. Truman, 1850. (Fabricated account of the Ezekiel Williams party's wanderings from Henry's fort on Henry's Fork of the Snake in 1810.)

De Lacy, Walter W. "A Trip up the South Snake River in 1863," *Contributions to the Historical Society of Montana,* I, (1876), 113–18.

Ferris, Warren A. *Life in the Rocky Mountains: A Diary of Wanderings on the Sources of the Rivers Missouri, Columbia, and Colorado from February 1830 to November 1835.* Ed. by Paul C. Phillips. Denver, F. A. Rosenstock–The Old West Publishing Co., 1940. (Ferris' journal was serialized much earlier in the *Western Literary Messenger* and the *Dallas Herald.*)

Franchère, Gabriel. *Narrative of a Voyage to the Northwest Coast of America in the Years 1811, 1812, 1813, and 1814: Or the First American Settlement on the Pacific.* Vol. VI in Reuben G. Thwaites (ed.), *Early Western Travels, 1747–1846.* (The first American edition, translated and edited by J. V. Huntington, was published in New York in 1854. The original edition of Franchère's narrative of the *Tonquin's* voyage to Fort Astoria, entitled *Relation d'un Voyage à la Côte du Nord-Ouest de l'Amerique Septentrionale dans les anneés 1810–1814,* was published in Montreal in 1820.)

Hamilton, W. T. *My Sixty Years on the Plains: Trapping, Trading, and Indian Fighting.* Ed. by Donald J. Berthrong. Norman, University of Oklahoma Press, 1960. (Originally published ca. 1904, ed. by E. T. Sieber.)

Hamp, Sidford. "Exploring the Yellowstone with Hayden, 1872: Diary of Sidford Hamp," ed. by Herbert O. Brayer, *Annals of Wyoming,* XIV (1942), 253–98.

Hunt, Wilson Price. "Journey of Mr. Hunt and His Companions from Saint Louis to the Mouth of the Columbia by a New Route Across the Rocky Mountains." In Philip A. Rollins (ed.), *The Discovery of the Oregon Trail,* Appendix A, 281–328. (Rollins' version is a retranslation into English of the original translation of Hunt's diary into French in *Nouvelles Annales des Voyages* [Paris, 1821], X.)

Irving, Washington. *The Adventures of Captain Bonneville U.S.A. in the Rocky Mountains and the Far West.* Vol. VIII, Geoffrey Crayon Edition. New York, G. P. Putnam and Sons, 1880. (Originally published as *The Rocky Mountains: Or, Scenes, Incidents, and Adventures in the Far West; Digested from the Journal of Capt. B. L. E. Bonneville.* 2 vols. Philadelphia, 1837. Republished in 1961 by the University of Oklahoma Press under the editorship of Edgeley W. Todd.)

———. *Astoria; or Anecdotes of an Enterprise Beyond the Rocky Mountains.* Vol. XIII, Geoffrey Crayon Edition. New York, G. P. Putnam and Sons, 1883. (First edition published in Philadelphia in 1836. Republished in 1964 by the University of Oklahoma Press under the editorship of Edgeley W. Todd.)

Jackson, Donald (ed.). *Letters of the Lewis and Clark Expedition, with Related Documents, 1783–1854*. Urbana, University of Illinois, 1962.

Jackson, William Henry. *Time Exposure: The Autobiography of William Henry Jackson*. New York, G. P. Putnam and Sons, 1940.

———, and Howard R. Driggs. *The Pioneer Photographer: Rocky Mountain Adventures with a Camera*. Yonkers-on-Hudson, N.Y., World Book Co., 1929.

James, Thomas. *Three Years Among the Indians and Mexicans*. Ed. by Walter B. Douglas. 2d ed. St. Louis, Missouri Historical Society, 1916. (First edition published in 1846.)

Leonard, Zenas. *Narrative of the Adventures of Zenas Leonard*. Clearfield, Pa., D. W. Moore, 1839. (Reprinted in W. F. Wagner [ed.], *Adventures of Zenas Leonard, Fur Trader and Trapper, 1831–1836*. Cleveland, The Burrows Brothers Company, 1904. Republished as *Adventures of Zenas Leonard, Fur Trader* in 1959 by the University of Oklahoma Press under the editorship of John C. Ewers.)

Marsh, James, B. *Four Years in the Rockies: Or the Adventures of Isaac P. Rose*. 2d ed. Columbus, Ohio, 1950. (First edition published in Newcastle, Pa., in 1884 by W. B. Thomas.)

Meek, Stephen Hall. *The Autobiography of a Mountain Man, 1805–1899*. Ed. by Arthur Woodward. Pasadena, Calif., 1948. (This work first appeared under the title "A Sketch of the Life of the First Pioneer" in *The Golden Era* [San Francisco] in April, 1885.)

Murie, Margaret E., and Olaus J. Murie. *Wapiti Wilderness*. New York, Alfred A. Knopf, 1966.

Parker, Samuel. *Journal of an Exploring Tour Beyond the*

Rocky Mountains under the Direction of the A.B.C.-F.M. in the Years 1835, '36, and '37. 3rd ed. Ithaca, N.Y., Mack, Andrus, and Woodruff, 1842. (First published in 1838.)

Paul, Elliot H. *Desperate Scenery.* New York, Random House, 1954. (Paul recalls the winter of 1910–11, when he worked in Jackson Hole for the construction company rebuilding Jackson Lake Dam.)

Quaife, M. M. (ed.). "Letters of John Ball, 1832–1833," *Mississippi Valley Historical Review,* V (March, 1919), 450–68. (As Nathaniel J. Wyeth's employee, Ball trapped in Jackson Hole during 1832 and 1833.)

Rollins, Philip Ashton (ed.). *The Discovery of the Oregon Trail: Robert Stuart's Narrative of His Overland Trip Eastward from Astoria in 1812–13; . . . An Account of the Tonquin's Voyage and of Events at Fort Astoria (1811–12); . . . Wilson Price Hunt's Diary of His Overland Trip Westward in 1811–12.* New York, Charles Scribner's Sons, 1935. (The main portion contains Stuart's journal and traveling memoranda. The anonymous account of the *Tonquin's* voyage and life at Fort Astoria and the redaction of Hunt's diary are included in the Appendix A, 267–328. A more recent work concerning Stuart is Kenneth A. Spaulding [ed.], *On the Oregon Trail: Robert Stuart's Journey of Discovery.* Norman, University of Oklahoma Press, 1953.)

Ross, Alexander. *Adventures of the First Settlers on the Oregon or Columbia River: Being a Narrative of the Expedition Fitted Out by John Jacob Astor, To Establish the "Pacific Fur Company"; with an account of some of the Indian tribes on the Coast of the Pacific.* Vol. VII in Reuben G. Thwaites (ed.), *Early Western*

Travels, 1748–1846. (First edition published in London in 1849 by Smith, Elder and Company.)

———. *The Fur Hunters of the Far West: A Narrative of Adventures in the Oregon and Rocky Mountains*. 2 vols. London, Smith, Elder, and Company, 1855. (Republished in 1956 and 1960 by the University of Oklahoma Press under the editorship of Kenneth A. Spaulding. Concerns Ross's employment with the North West and Hudson's Bay companies.)

Russell, Osborne. *Journal of a Trapper, or Nine Years in the Rocky Mountains, 1834–1843*. Ed. by Aubrey L. Haines. 3rd ed. Portland, Oregon Historical Society, 1955.

Thwaites, Reuben G. (ed.). *Early Western Travels, 1748–1846*. 32 vols. Cleveland, The Arthur H. Clark Company, 1904–1907. (Annotated reprints of rare contemporary accounts by trappers and explorers.)

———. *Original Journals of the Lewis and Clark Expeditions, 1804–1806*. 7 vols. New York, Dodd, Mead and Company, 1904–1905.

Townsend, John K. *Narrative of a Journey across the Rocky Mountains to the Columbia River*. Vol. XXI in Reuben G. Thwaites (ed.), *Early Western Travels, 1748–1846*. (First edition published in Philadelphia in 1839 by H. Perkins. Recounts Nathaniel J. Wyeth's second [1834] expedition.)

Victor, Frances Fuller. *The River of the West: Life and Adventures in the Rocky Mountains and Oregon, Embracing Events in the Life-Time of a Mountain-Man and Pioneer with the Early History of the North-Western Slope*. Hartford, Conn., Columbian Book Company, 1870. (Based on the reminiscences of trapper Joseph Meek.)

Waterhouse, Benjamin, and John B. Wyeth. *Oregon; or A Short History of a Long Journey from the Atlantic Ocean to the Region of the Pacific by Land*. Vol. XXI in Reuben G. Thwaites (ed.), *Early Western Travels, 1748–1846*. (First edition published in Cambridge, Mass., in 1833. Unsympathetic account of Nathaniel J. Wyeth's first [1832] expedition. John B. Wyeth, Nathaniel's cousin, accompanied the 1832 expedition as far as Pierre's Hole, then returned to Cambridge, where Dr. Waterhouse, an avowed enemy of western emigration, encouraged him to publish his narrative as a means of discouraging people from going west. Passages written in the first person by John Wyeth are neutral in tone. Waterhouse's third-person inserts, however, are noticeably slanted and obviously not based on first-hand experience.)

Webb, Vanderbilt (ed.). *Mr. John D. Rockefeller, Jr.'s Proposed Gift of Land for the National Park System in Wyoming: History of the Snake River Land Company and of the efforts to Preserve the Jackson Hole Country for the Nation*. N.p., n.d. (Foreword by Webb, president of the Snake River Land Company. Contains letters addressed to Wilford W. Neilson, editor of the *Jackson's Hole Courier*, and printed in the *Courier* during the spring of 1933. The letters are from Horace M. Albright, director of the National Park Service; Harold P. Fabian, vice president of the Snake River Land Company; and J. H. Rayburn, president of Teton Investment Company.)

Wilson, Elijah Nicholas, with Howard R. Driggs. *The White Indian Boy: The Story of Uncle Nick Among the Shoshones*. Rev. ed., Yonkers-on-Hudson, World

Book Co., 1919. ("Uncle Nick" was an early settler in Jackson Hole.)

Wister, Owen. *Owen Wister Out West: His Journals and Letters*. Ed. by Fanny Kemble Wister. Chicago, University of Chicago Press, 1958. (Miss Wister is Owen's daughter. Her introduction recalls her summers in Jackson Hole in 1911 and 1912.)

Wyeth, Nathaniel J. "Journal of 1832." In Archer B. Hulbert (ed.), *The Call of the Columbia: Iron Men and Saints Take the Oregon Trail*. Denver and Colorado Springs, Denver Public Library and Stewart Commission of Colorado College, 1934.

UNPUBLISHED MANUSCRIPTS

Hebard, Grace Raymond. Manuscript Collection. University of Wyoming Archives, Laramie.

Jackson Hole Manuscript Collection. University of Wyoming Archives.

Leigh, Richard. Manuscript Collection. University of Wyoming Archives.

National Park Service Files. National Archives, Washington, D.C.

Owen, William O. Manuscript Collection. University of Wyoming Archives.

Simpson, William L. Manuscript Collection. University of Wyoming Archives.

ARTICLES

Albright, Horace M. "The Glory of Jackson Hole," *New York Times Magazine*, January 21, 1945, 22–23.

Boyd, Katharine. "Heard About Jackson Hole?" *Atlantic Monthly*, CLXXV (April, 1945), 102–106.

Boyer, David S. "Wyoming: High, Wide, and Windy," *National Geographic Magazine*, CXXIX (April, 1966), 554–92.

Brant, Irving. "The Fight over Jackson Hole," *The Nation*, CLXI (July 7, 1945), 13–14.

Burt, Struthers. "The Battle of Jackson's Hole," *The Nation*, CXXII (March 3, 1926), 225–27.

———. "Jackson Hole and the Tetons," *Union Pacific Magazine*, III (July, 1924), 5.

Chapman, William McK. "Jackson Hole and the Grand Tetons," *American Legion Magazine* (July, 1965), 18–21, 48–49.

Craighead, Frank, and John Craighead. "Cloud Gardens in the Tetons," *National Geographic Magazine*, XCIII (June, 1948), 811–30.

———. "Wildlife Adventuring in the Tetons," *National Geographic Magazine*, CIX (January, 1956), 1–36.

Duncan, John B. "An Elk Hunt in Jackson Hole," *The Tee pee Book*, II (December, 1916), 8–9, 15–20.

Irland, Frederic. "The Wyoming Game Stronghold," *Scribner's Magazine*, XXXIV (September, 1903), 259–76.

"The Jackson Hole Country of Wyoming: What the Proposed Addition to the Yellowstone Is Like," *Scientific American*, CXVIII (March 30, 1918), 272.

Jeffers, LeRoy. "From the Mountains of Montana to the Tetons of Wyoming: Strolls Through a Region Whose Scenic Beauties Are Menaced by the Mailed Fist of Commercialism," *Scientific American*, CXXII (April 3, 1920), 364, 375–76.

Johnson, Lynda Bird. "I See America First," *National Geographic Magazine*, CXXVIII (December, 1965), 874–904.

Jones, J. R. "Jackson Hole," *Union Pacific Magazine,* III (July, 1924), 31–34.

Judge, Frances. "The Fun of Living," *Naturalist,* XII (Spring, 1961). (Recounts the dances and other entertainment that were a part of the author's childhood in Jackson Hole.)

Langford, Nathaniel P. "The Ascent of Mount Hayden: A New Chapter in Western Discovery," *Scribner's Monthly,* VI (June, 1873), 129–37.

Lipscomb, James. "Night of the One-Eyed Devils," *Sports Illustrated,* XXII (June 21, 1965), 64–77.

———. "72 Hours of Terror," *Sports Illustrated,* XXII (June 14, 1965), 86–104.

McFarland, J. Horace. "The Yellowstone Park Question," *Outlook,* CXXV (July 28, 1920), 578. (Letter to the editors.)

Milne, Lorus J., and Margery J. Milne. "Close-up of Our Wildlife," *New York Times Magazine,* August 22, 1948, 10–11. (Pictorial study of the Jackson Hole Wildlife Park, now maintained by the National Park Service as a buffalo pasture.)

Owen, William O. "The Ascent of the Grand Teton," *Outing,* XXXVIII (June, 1901), 302–307.

Reardan, J. D. "Up Grand Teton," *Outing,* LXVII (December, 1915), 267–78.

Sutton, Horace. "Grand Tetons or Bust," *Saturday Review* (June 18, 1955), 36–38. (Tourist account.)

Villard, Oswald Garrison. "A Park, a Man, and the Rest of Us," *Survey,* LV (February 1, 1926), 542–44.

Wallace, Dillon. "Saddle and Camp in the Rockies: The End of the Trail," *Outing,* LVIII (June, 1911), 319–33. (Illustrated with elk photographs by Steve Leek of Jackson Hole.)

————. "Saddle and Camp in the Rockies: The Tragedy of the Elk," *Outing*, LVIII (May, 1911), 187–201.

NEWSPAPERS

Grand Teton, Jackson, Wyo.
Jackson Hole Guide, Jackson, Wyo.
Jackson's Hole Courier, Jackson, Wyo.
New York Times.
Wyoming State Journal, Lander, Wyo.

PERSONAL INTERVIEWS

Albright, Horace M. October 18, 1967, New York, N.Y.
Bill, Harthon L. March 28, 1966, Washington, D.C. (Mr. Bill spent three and a half years during the early 1960's as superintendent of Grand Teton National Park. He later became deputy director of the National Park Service.)
Fabian, Harold P. Aug. 1, 1968, Moose, Wyo.

MUSEUMS

Fur Trade Museum, Moose, Wyo.
Jackson Hole Museum, Jackson, Wyo.
Menor's Ferry Museum, Moose, Wyo.
Mountain Climbing Museum, Jenny Lake, Wyo.
Wyoming State Museum, Cheyenne, Wyo.

Secondary Sources

BIBLIOGRAPHIES

Wagner, Henry R. *The Plains and the Rockies: A Bibliography of Original Narratives of Travel and Adventure, 1800–1865.* Ed. by Charles R. Camp. 3rd ed. Columbus, Ohio, Long's College Book Company, 1953.

Withington, Mary C. A *Catalogue of Manuscripts in the Collection of Western Americana in the Yale University Library*. New Haven, Conn., Yale University Press, 1952. (William Robertson Coe Collection.)

Bancroft, Hubert Howe. *History of Nevada, Colorado, and Wyoming, 1540–1888*. Vol. XXV in *The Works of Hubert Howe Bancroft*. San Francisco, The History Company, 1890. (Mrs. Frances Fuller Victor wrote nearly all of the section on Wyoming.)

Coutant, C. G. *The History of Wyoming from the Earliest Known Discoveries*. Laramie, Wyo., Chaplin, Spafford, and Mathison, 1899. (This is Vol. I of a never completed set which was to include three volumes. Covers up to 1869.)

Larson, T. A. *History of Wyoming*. Lincoln, University of Nebraska Press, 1965. (Concentrates on the period from 1865 to the present.)

Lavender, David. *The American Heritage History of the Great West*. Ed. by Alvin M. Josephy, Jr. New York, Simon and Schuster, 1965.

Wyoming: A Guide to Its History, Highways, and People. New York, Oxford University Press, 1941. (Works Progress Administration, Federal Writers Project.)

Alter, J. Cecil. *James Bridger: Trapper, Frontiersman, Scout, and Guide*. Salt Lake City, Shepard Book Company, 1925. (Includes a biographical sketch, "James Bridger," by Major General Granville M. Dodge. Republished in 1962 and 1967 by the University of Oklahoma Press.)

Caesar, Gene. *King of the Mountain Men: The Life of Jim Bridger*. New York, Dutton, 1961.

Fryxell, Fritiof. "Prospector of Jackson Hole." In *Campfire Tales of Jackson Hole*. Moose, Wyo., Grand Teton Natural History Association, 1960. Pp. 47–51. About "Uncle Jack" Davis.)

Hafen, LeRoy R. (ed.). *The Mountain Men and the Fur Trade of the Far West*. 4 vols. Glendale, Calif., The Arthur H. Clark Company, 1965–66.

Harris, Burton. *John Colter: His Years in the Rockies*. New York, Charles Scribner's Sons, 1952.

Jackson, Clarence S. *Picture Maker of the Old West: William H. Jackson*. New York, Charles Scribner's Sons, 1947.

Johnson, Allen, *et al.* (eds.). *Dictionary of American Biography*. 22 vols. New York, Charles Scribner's Sons, 1928–58.

Morgan, Dale. *Jedediah Smith and the Opening of the West*. Indianapolis, Bobbs-Merrill, 1953.

Mumey, Nolie. *The Life of Jim Baker, 1818–1898: Trapper, Scout, Guide, and Indian Fighter*. Denver, The World Press, 1931. (Not reliable.)

Potts, Merlin K. "John Colter: The Discovery of Jackson Hole and the Yellowstone." In *Campfire Tales of Jackson Hole*. Moose, Wyo., Grand Teton Natural History Association, 1960. Pp. 4–10.

Russell, Isaac K., with Howard R. Driggs. *Hidden Heroes of the Rockies*. Yonkers-on-Hudson, World Book Company, 1923. (For children.)

Sullivan, Maurice S. *Jedediah Smith: Trader and Trailbreaker*. New York, Press of the Pioneers, Inc., 1936.

Sunder, John E. *Bill Sublette: Mountain Man*. Norman, University of Oklahoma Press, 1959.

Tilden, Freeman. *Following the Frontier with F. Jay Haynes, Pioneer Photographer of the Old West.* New York, Alfred A. Knopf, 1964. (Shows some of Haynes's best shots of the Tetons and Jackson Hole.)

Vestal, Stanley. *Jim Bridger, Mountain Man.* New York, W. Morrow, 1946.

Vinton, Stallo. *John Colter: Discoverer of Yellowstone Park.* New York, E. Eberstadt, 1926.

SPECIAL STUDIES

Albright, Horace M., and Frank J. Taylor. *"Oh Ranger":* *A Book about the National Parks.* New York, Dodd, Mead and Company, 1934.

Anderson, Chester C. *The Elk of Jackson Hole: A Review of Jackson Hole Elk Studies.* Wyoming Game and Fish Commission *Bulletin* 10. Cheyenne, 1958.

Bakeless, John. *Lewis and Clark, Partners in Discovery.* New York, W. Morrow, 1947.

Barry, J. Neilson. "John Colter's Map of 1814," *Wyoming Annals,* X (July, 1938), 100–10.

Bartlett, Richard A. *Great Surveys of the American West.* Norman, University of Oklahoma Press, 1962.

Beal, Merrill D. *The Story of Man in Yellowstone.* Caldwell, Idaho, Caxton Printers, Ltd., 1949.

Bonney, Orrin H., and Lorraine G. Bonney. *Bonney's Guide: Jackson's Hole and Grand Teton National Park.* Rev. ed. Houston, 1961.

Brown, Roland W., Jr. (ed.). *Souvenir History of Jackson Hole.* Salt Lake City, 1924. (Written by seventh- and eighth-grade pupils in the Jackson Public School, 1923–24.)

Butler, James D. "John Colter," *Magazine of American*

History, XII (July, 1884), 83–86. (Letters to the editors.)

Chittenden, Hiram M. *The American Fur Trade of the Far West*. 2 vols. Stanford, Calif., Academic Reprints, 1954. (First edition published in New York in 1902 by F. P. Harper.)

——. *The Yellowstone National Park, Historical and Descriptive*. Cincinnati, Robert Clarke Company, 1895. (Revised and republished as *The Yellowstone National Park* in 1964 [5th ed.] by the University of Oklahoma Press under the editorship of Richard A. Bartlett.)

Christopherson, Edmund. *Behold the Grand Tetons: The Exciting Story of the Jackson Hole Country*. Missoula, Mont., 1961. (Brief pamphlet for tourist-reader.)

Dale, Harrison Clifford. *The Ashley-Smith Explorations and the Discovery of the Central Route to the Pacific, 1822–1829*. Rev. ed. Glendale, Calif., The Arthur H. Clark Company, 1941. (First published in 1918. Includes portions of the original journals of William Ashley, Jedediah Smith, and Harrison G. Rogers.)

DeVoto, Bernard. *Across the Wide Missouri*. Boston, Houghton-Mifflin Company, 1947. (Fur trade era.)

——. *The Year of Decision, 1846*. Boston, Little, Brown and Company, 1943.

Driggs, B. W. *History of Teton Valley Idaho*. Caldwell, Idaho, Caxton Printers, Ltd., 1926.

Eaton, W. Clement. "Nathaniel Wyeth's Oregon Expeditions," *Pacific Historical Review*, IV (1935), 101–13.

Ellison, William Henry. "From Pierre's Hole to Monterey: A Chapter in the Adventures of George Nidever, Pioneer of the Rocky Mountains and of California," *Pacific Historical Review*, I (1932), 82–102.

Fabian, Josephine C. *Jackson Hole: How to Discover and Enjoy It.* Salt Lake City, 1949.

Frost, Donald M. "Notes on General Ashley, the Overland Trail, and South Pass," *Proceedings of the American Antiquarian Society,* LIV (October, 1944), 161–312.

Fryxell, Fritiof. "The Story of Deadman's Bar." In *Campfire Tales of Jackson Hole.* Moose, Wyo., Grand Teton Natural History Association, 1960. Pp. 43–46.

———. *The Teton Peaks and Their Ascents.* [Jackson Hole, Wyo., Crandall Studios, 1932.]

———. *The Tetons: Interpretations of a Mountain Landscape.* Berkeley, University of California Press, 1938.

Fryxell, Roald. "The Affair at Cunningham's Cabin." In *Campfire Tales of Jackson Hole.* Moose, Wyo., Grand Teton Natural History Association, 1960. Pp. 43–46.

Ghent, W. J. "A Sketch of John Colter," *Wyoming Annals,* X (July, 1938), 111–16.

Goetzmann, William H. *Army Exploration in the American West, 1803–1863.* New Haven, Conn., Yale University Press, 1959.

———. *Exploration and Empire: The Explorer and the Scientist in the Winning of the American West.* New York, Alfred A. Knopf, 1966.

Graham, Gordon. *A Study of the Economy of Jackson, Wyoming: November 1, 1966.* Jackson, 1966. (Prepared for Jackson Hole Chamber of Commerce.)

Hagen, Harold K. *A Fishing Guide to Jackson Hole.* Cheyenne, Wyo., Pioneer Printing Company, 1954.

Harmston, Floyd K., *et al. A Study of the Resources, People, and Economy of Teton County, Wyoming.* Laramie, 1959.

Harry, Bryan. *Teton Trails.* Moose, Wyo., Grand Teton Natural History Association, 1963.

Hayden, Elizabeth Wied. *From Trapper to Tourist in Jackson Hole*. 2nd rev. ed. Jackson, Wyo., 1963. (First published in 1957. Not fully reliable. Poor footnoting.)

Heffelfinger, C. H. "John Colter, the Man Who Turned Back," *Washington Historical Quarterly*, XXVI (July, 1935), 192–6.

Hough, Donald. *The Cocktail Hour in Jackson Hole*. New York, W. W. Norton and Company, 1956. (Native's long winters in the valley.)

———. *Snow Above Town*. New York, W. W. Norton and Company, 1943.

Hulbert, Archer B. (ed.). *The Call of the Columbia: Iron Men and Saints Take the Oregon Trail*. Denver and Colorado Springs, Denver Public Library and Stewart Commission of Colorado College, 1934.

——— and Dorothy P. Hulbert (eds.). *The Oregon Crusade: Across Land and Sea to Oregon*. Denver and Colorado Springs, Denver Public Library and Stewart Commission of Colorado College, 1935.

———. *Where Rolls the Oregon: Prophet and Pessimist Look Northwest*. Denver and Colorado Springs, Denver Public Library and Stewart Commission of Colorado College, 1933.

Ise, John. *Our National Park Policy: A Critical History*. Baltimore, Johns Hopkins University Press, 1961.

Jackson, William T. "The Creation of Yellowstone National Park," *Mississippi Valley Historical Review*, XXIX (September, 1942), 187–206.

———. "Governmental Exploration of the Upper Yellowstone, 1871," *Pacific Historical Review*, XI (June, 1942), 187–99.

———. "The Washburn-Doane Expedition into the Upper

Yellowstone, 1870," *Pacific Historical Review*, X (June, 1941), 189–208.

Judge, Frances. "Mountain River Men: The Story of Menor's Ferry." In *Campfire Tales of Jackson Hole*. Moose, Wyo., Grand Teton Natural History Association, 1960. Pp. 52–58.

Koch, P. "Discovery of the Yellowstone National Park: A Chapter of Early Exploration in the Rocky Mountains," *Magazine of American History*, XI (1884), 497–512.

Lavender, David. *The Big Divide*. Garden City, N.Y., Doubleday and Company, 1948.

———. *The Fist in the Wilderness*. Garden City, N.Y., Doubleday and Company, 1964.

Mattes, Merrill J. "Behind the Legend of Colter's Hell: The Early Exploration of Yellowstone National Park," *Mississippi Valley Historical Review*, XXXVI (September, 1949), 251–82.

———. *Jackson Hole: Crossroads of the Western Fur Trade, 1807–1840*. N.p., n.d. (Reprints of "Jackson Hole, Crossroads of the Western Fur Trade, 1807–1829," *Pacific Northwest Quarterly*, XXXVII [April, 1946], 87–108, and "Jackson Hole, Crossroads of the Western Fur Trade, 1830–1840," *Pacific Northwest Quarterly*, XXXIX [January, 1948], 3–32.)

Mumey, Nolie. *The Teton Mountains: Their History and Tradition*. Denver, The Artcraft Press, 1947.

Murie, Olaus J. *The Elk of North America*. Harrisburg, Pa., and Washington, D.C., Stackpole Company and Wildlife Management Institute, 1951.

Ortenburger, Leigh. *A Climber's Guide to the Teton Range*. Rev. ed. San Francisco, Sierra Club, 1965.

Phillips, Paul C. *The Fur Trade.* 2 vols. Norman, University of Oklahoma Press, 1961.

Pomeroy, Earl. *In Search of the Golden West: The Tourist in Western America.* New York, Alfred A. Knopf, 1957.

Potts, Merlin K. "The Doane Expedition of 1876–77: Fort Ellis, Montana Territory to Fort Hall, Idaho." In *Campfire Tales of Jackson Hole.* Moose, Wyo., Grand Teton Natural History Association, 1960. Pp. 20–37. (Potts consulted a copy of Doane's original manuscript on file in the park headquarters library, Grand Teton National Park, Moose.)

———. "The Mountain Men in Jackson Hole." In *Campfire Tales of Jackson Hole.* Moose, Wyo., Grand Teton Natural History Association, 1960. Pp. 11–19.

Reed, John C. "Geology of the Teton Range." In Leigh Ortenburger, *A Climber's Guide to the Teton Range,* 321–29.

Russell, Carl P. "Trapper Trails to the Sisk-ke-dee," *Annals of Wyoming,* XVII (July, 1945), 88–105.

Sandoz, Mari. *The Beaver Men: Spearheads of Empire.* New York, Hastings House, 1964.

Stone, Elizabeth. *Uinta County: Its Place in History.* Laramie, Wyo., Laramie Printing Company, 1924.

Trail, E. B. "The Life and Adventures of John Colter," *Old Travois Trails,* II (January–February, 1942).

U.S. Department of the Interior, National Park Service. *Grand Teton National Park, Wyoming.* Rev. ed. Washington, D.C., Government Printing Office, 1964. (Pamphlet given to each visitor as he enters the park.)

Van Every, Dale. *The Final Challenge: The American Frontier, 1804–1845.* New York, W. Morrow, 1964.

FICTION

Burt, Struthers. *The Delectable Mountains*. New York, Charles Scribner's Sons, 1927. (Mentions the damming of Jackson Hole's waterways.)

Carrighar, Sally. *One Day at Teton Marsh*. New York, Alfred A. Knopf, 1947. (Republished in New York in 1965 by Pyramid Book Company. Nature writing. Later made into a motion picture.)

Fisher, Vardis. *Mountain Man*. New York, W. Morrow, 1965.

Guthrie, A. B., Jr. *The Big Sky*. New York, William Sloane Associates, 1947. (Republished in New York in 1965 in Pocket Cardinal Edition. The classic account of an eastern boy who runs away from home to become a trapper and mountain man. A movie based on the book was filmed in Jackson Hole.)

Manfred, Frederick. *Lord Grizzly*. New York, McGraw-Hill Book Company, 1954.

Rogers, W. P. *Oldtimer of the Jackson Hole Country of Wyoming: A Story of Mountain Men for Men Only*. Dallas, Warlick Press, 1964.

Stewart, William G. D. *Altowan, or Incidents of Life and Adventures in the Rocky Mountains by an Amateur Traveller*. Ed. by James W. Webb. 2 vols. New York, Harper and Brothers Company, 1846. (Stewart had accompanied roving trapper bands through the West.)

Wister, Owen. *The Virginian: A Horseman of the Plains*. Pocket Cardinal Edition. New York, 1964. (First published in New York in 1902 by the Macmillan Company.)

MAPS

U.S. Department of the Interior, Geological Survey. *Driggs, Idaho, Quadrangle.* Scale 1:250,000. Washington, D.C., 1955. (Originally prepared by the Army Map Service, Corps of Engineers, U.S. Army.)

———. *Topographic Map of the Grand Teton National Park, Teton County, Wyoming.* Scale 1:62,500. Washington, D.C., 1948.

258

INDEX